If there's anyone out there who understands better the digital component of our Google world than Phil Cooke, I don't know who it is. *The Last TV Evangelist* might be better titled, *The First Yellow Brick Road to Our Digital Future.* You'd be wise to get on it quick.

LEONARD SWEET
DREW THEOLOGICAL SCHOOL, GEORGE FOX UNIVERSITY

Every generation needs a grumpy prophet, and Phil Cooke has ably volunteered. It's easy to cast aspersion on every form of media, but the fact that Phil is examining his own house with such candor and expert articulation makes this book entirely worth the read. Sometimes the loudest guy in the room is right.

TODD KOMARNICKI
PRODUCER OF "ELF" AND AUTHOR OF WAR, FAMINE, & FREE

The gospel message is sacred. The medium isn't. Every generation needs to find new ways of creatively communicating the truth. And every generation needs media-prophets like Phil Cooke. *The Last TV Evangelist* is a must-read for anyone who is tired of living within the comfortable confines of the Christian Bubble, as Phil calls it, and really wants their voice to be heard in the culture-at-large. Bravo!

MARK BATTERSON
LEAD PASTOR OF NATIONAL COMMUNITY CHURCH
AND AUTHOR OF WILD GOOSE CHASE

Phil, with total honesty and clarity, gives great insight into the world of religious media. For anyone involved with Christian content or who desires to understand religious media, this is a must read. *The Last TV Evangelist* will be invaluable for generations to come.

TONY THOMOPOULOS
FORMER PRESIDENT OF ABC BROADCAST GROUP AND
FORMER CHAIRMAN OF UNITED ARTISTS PICTURES

In the struggle for connecting with the hearts and minds of the American public in the arena of the "new digital media," *The Last TV Evangelist* will become the battlefield instruction manual for those who are attempting to successfully utilize this quickly evolving medium. It is rare to find a book like this that so succinctly weaves together theory and practical application.

ARTHUR ANDERSON
CO-PRODUCER OF MISSION IMPOSSIBLE III, PAYCHECK,
WINDTALKERS, AND BMW FILMS: THE HOSTAGE

This is Phil Cooke's best book. It does not just point out toxic faith on the air, it has solutions. Phil is brilliant and we are changing some things at NewLife Live because of *The Last TV Evangelist*. It is a new media world, and Phil does a great job of telling us how to reach into it. If you are behind the times, this book will help you catch up. Now.

STEVE ARTERBURN
FOUNDER AND CHAIRMAN OF NEWLIFE MINISTRIES

We love *The Last TV Evangelist*, but if we published it, we would jeopardize our relationship with too many TV ministries.

A MAJOR RELIGIOUS PUBLISHER

THE LAST
TV
EVANGELIST

THE LAST
✝
TV
EVANGELIST

**WHY THE NEXT GENERATION
COULDN'T CARE LESS ABOUT
RELIGIOUS MEDIA
➤➤ AND WHY IT MATTERS ◄◄**

PHIL
COOKE

Conversant Media Group

Published by Conversant Media Group, Huntington Beach, CA.
www.ConversantMediaGroup.com

FIRST EDITION

Cover design and layout by Ralph Polendo Jr. (rpjrdesign.com)

Library of Congress Cataloging-in-Publication Data is available upon request.

ISBN 978-0-9819515-0-8

Printed in the United States of America.

TABLE OF CONTENTS

In the fall of 1972, I was a freshman in college majoring in music. I had grown up as a preacher's kid, and my only talent as far as I could tell was the ability to play the piano—although not very well. But this was college, and I had to declare something, so music it was. As I unpacked my suitcase in the dormitory, some Super-8 film reels I had shot in high school fell out on the floor.

I had a group of crazy high school buddies back in Charlotte, North Carolina who loved making amateur movies about gangsters, spacemen, monsters, soldiers, and more. Rod Carlson, who lived in the dorm room next door, picked up the reels and mentioned that if I was interested, he could take me over to the university film department and show me how to edit them. (I was so ignorant about filmmaking, the thought of actually cutting the film had never occurred to me.)

So later that night we went to the small and ill-equipped film department and started cutting. The professor, Dan Dunkelberger, was also there working on a project. After a few hours of leaning over the film splicer, professor Dunkelberger walked over to us and said, "I've been watching some of your film scenes, and to be honest, I have students that have been taking years of film classes and still don't do this well. Would you mind letting me show your film in class tomorrow?"

I was surprised, but said that if I could sit on the back row to see their reaction, then absolutely.

The next morning I bashfully walked into the classroom with about 25 older students and sat in the back as they threaded the projector and showed my little movie. Believe me when I tell you it wasn't much. We were strictly amateurs and had never even considered that this might eventually be a career choice. But when the lights came up, the students started talking about it. The movie wasn't great, but people mentioned camera angles, story points, and asked questions about different aspects of the production.

As I sat there in stunned silence, I had the only crystal clear epiphany I've ever had in my life. To be honest, I don't think I've ever had such a profound moment since. The class discussion began receding into the background of my mind as the thought occurred to me that *if I can do something with a film camera that will make people talk like this, then that is exactly what I'm supposed to do with my life.*

I walked out of that class, went straight to the registrar's office, and changed my major to the Communication Arts Department.

That was 1972, and nearly four decades and 40 countries later, I've never looked back.

Had professor Dunkelberger not noticed my little film, I might be playing the piano in a church (or seedy bar) somewhere in the Midwest. Dan—a man who himself was an early pioneer in faith-based film—retired that year, but a long time later, I had the opportunity to thank him. When I met him years later in California, I told him the impact he had on my career, and we discussed the remarkable difference one person can have on someone's life.

This book is for Dan. Because one person is all it takes. As you read the following pages, keep that in mind.

– Phil Cooke

INTRODUCTION

THERE'S A HUGE SHIFT GOING ON IN MEDIA. TEN OR FIFTEEN YEARS FROM NOW, WE'LL HAVE THE PERSPECTIVE TO SEE WHAT A BIG SHIFT IT WAS AND HOW MUCH IT CHANGED OUR LIVES. WE'LL BE ABLE TO UNDERSTAND THE UNEXPECTED RAMIFICATIONS OF THIS SHIFT. BUT FOR NOW, IT'S OFTEN A SERIES OF MUNDANE CHANGES THAT ARE SLOWLY WEANING OUR ATTENTION FROM MAINSTREAM BROADCAST TELEVISION.

– JAMES LEWIN, *THE SHIFT TO DIGITAL MEDIA*

The idea for this book was born a number of years ago when a friend of mine, who runs one of the largest traditional Christian television networks, reluctantly shared with me the results of a research study the organization had just completed. The results of the study indicated the reason the network's audience supported them financially wasn't because they liked the programming but because they liked the "idea" of Christian broadcasting. Indeed, my friend understood the viewers actually liked very little of what they saw at the time. In other words, they believed that people in every community in America – and probably the world – should have the opportunity to hear the Christian message through the medium of television. Therefore, they were willing to financially support the *mission*, even though they disliked the *results*.

NAVIGATING THE DIGITAL DIVIDE

It's hard not to agree with that research study. Since I began working in religious and non-profit media many years ago,

I haven't cared for much of what I've heard or seen – either on radio or television. Don't get me wrong, I applaud the efforts of all the well intentioned people who believe in using the media to share a message of faith and hope with the culture. The problem is most of them just haven't done it very well. I am not judging their motives or their hearts, but simply critiquing the impact (or lack thereof) most Christian broadcasting has actually had on the culture. And keep in mind, I put myself in this group. As a preacher's kid, I've been involved behind the scenes in ministry all of my life, and in religious media since 1973.

In 2008, after writing the book *Branding Faith*, someone at a conference asked me what my own brand story was, and I responded that it was about "helping people discover their voice." Most readers of my books, magazine articles or blog (philcooke.com), as well as many clients over the years would probably agree. I want to help the Church recapture its influence in the culture. As a result, the vast majority of our work at Cooke Pictures, my media consultancy and production company, is asking our clients to change their perspective on the media. It doesn't matter if you're a pastor, ministry leader, filmmaker, artist, writer – whatever. We believe in engaging the culture in new and innovative ways, and are relentless in the pursuit of that goal.

After all, culture changes, trends change, and people change. Study biology and you'll discover that if living things aren't growing and changing – they're dying.

Still water gets stagnant pretty quickly.

At Cooke Pictures, our clients include some of the largest and most effective non-profits and media ministries in the world – and from time to time, some of the *least* effective. For the most part, we are hired to help them get to the next level – even when that means facing some uncomfortable truths about how they've created radio and TV programs in the past. But in the majority of cases, I find that clients are willing to go under the knife. They know the stakes are high, and are committed to making a difference – even if it means a paradigm shift.

However, many other traditional religious media organizations aren't that forward thinking. Many are happy to continue producing the same radio and TV programming they have always produced. They don't want to think about perception or branding or culture or connection or it would seem – results. While a few are driven by ego or money, I've discovered for the most part, these are good people with noble intentions, but held back by outdated and out of touch strategies that need to be ushered into the digital age.

Religious media organizations run the gamut from simply missing the mark, or not understanding how to engage the culture, to major organizations who have it completely backwards; ministries that started out with a great mission, and somewhere along the line, replaced that *mission* with *money*. They spend their time talking about fundraising rather than ministry opportunities, because in most cases, they've grown to the point that they must spend most of their efforts on raising the money in order to make the ministry happen.

The tail wags the dog indeed.

CHANGE IS HAPPENING

As I write this book, *The Wall Street Journal* reported that the median age for television viewers reached 50 for the first time in history. This is literally shaking up the advertising and entertainment industries because the coveted 18-49 demographic can no longer be counted on to tune in to prime time television. The research from Magna Global, a media services firm, indicates the median age per network breaks down like this:

CBS – 54
ABC – 50 (Walt Disney owned)
NBC – 49
ABC – 48
FOX – 42

This means that 18-49 year olds are opting for other forms of entertainment, such as videogames, the Internet, and mobile phones. TV has lost it's historic position as the *first screen* for the younger crowd.

> **LAST YEAR I BOUGHT SEASON TWO OF ABC'S 'LOST' ON DVD. THIS YEAR, I'M CATCHING UP ON MISSED EPISODES ON THE INTERNET.**
> — JENNIFER WOODARD MADERAZO, PBS'S *MEDIASHIFT*

While individual programs continue to reach younger audiences, the results are in – and it's all about new media. If you want to reach a new generation, putting all your eggs in the traditional media basket is a mistake.

IT'S ABOUT CONNECTION

The new media world is about connection, community, and conversation. It's about being networked. In that world, small things matter. As a result, the way the next generation views media is undergoing a dramatic shift.

For instance, when I want news, I know where to go. As I'll detail later in the book, I have a routine that includes multiple daily newspapers, cable news channels, and RSS fees on my computer and mobile phone. Essentially, I go to where the news is waiting.

But being connected is so integral to a new generation, *they expect the news to find them.* What we call "push" technology has changed the flow of information. After all, today's young people are constantly connected via online social networks, texting, mobile phones, e-mail and more, leading them to assume if it's important, it will come to them. That revelation alone should shake communicators to the core.

> **THERE IS ONE OVERRIDING, SIMPLE, BUT POWERFUL MESSAGE FOR ALL TWENTY-FIRST-CENTURY MARKETING, MEDIA, AND ADVERTISING EXECUTIVES: INSIGHT ABOUT CONSUMERS IS THE CURRENCY THAT TRUMPS ALL OTHERS.**
> – CHRISTOPHER VOLLMER, *ALWAYS ON: ADVERTISING, MARKETING, AND MEDIA IN AN ERA OF CONSUMER CONTROL*

Change isn't coming – it's here. Consider this book as an insider's, behind-the-scenes glimpse of that change. It's a look at the inner-workings of traditional religious media, and how we arrived at this challenging crossroads. It's an examination of the stuff we sell on the air, the crazy product offers and "Jesus junk," the direct mail campaigns that fund it, the stress it puts on ministry leaders, and the less than flattering perception of Christians it leaves with the audience at large.

We'll look at how we got to this point and how I believe we can get out; what are the possibilities for moving to the next level, and the consequences of not acting now. This is a 30,000 foot view. It isn't an owner's manual on how to operate an iPhone, or move from Microsoft Word to Google online office applications. It won't teach you how to keep a family photo album on Photobucket, or make long distance calls through Skype. Rather, it's a much bigger view of the radical shift that's happening in the world today that will – and should – change everything you know about communicating your message.

Throughout the book I'll be using examples from my own experience, information from secular media, as well as advertising and marketing. I'm sensitive to the idea of applying advertising and marketing principles to the world of religion. There are many critics, and in my book *Branding Faith* I dealt with many of those issues. However, I continue to use advertising and branding techniques as a key reference point because of all media, advertising is focused on *reaching an audience and motivating change*. Entertainment is great, and I love a good movie or captivating television program, but ultimately, religious programmers are motivated toward *change*. Whether it's through a website, traditional radio or TV programming, or a print campaign, we're hopefully inspiring people to a fundamental transformation in their lives.

If motivating your audience toward change and transformation is the goal, then there is enormous benefit from understanding the power and principles of effective advertising and branding.

The stakes are high. This is way beyond a pastor's egotistical dream to be on television, write a bestselling book, or the desire for fame or fortune. As we move into the 21st century, this is about the Christian community's impact on the culture, and how the general public thinks about Christians. It's about effectiveness and the ability to change people's thinking.

Buckle up. It will be an interesting ride.

CHAPTER ONE
HOW WE ARRIVED *HERE*

> WE HAVE CREATED A PHENOMENAL SUBCULTURE WITH OUR OWN MEDIA, ENTERTAINMENT, EDUCATIONAL SYSTEM, AND POLITICAL HIERARCHY SO THAT WE HAVE THE SENSE THAT WE'RE DOING A LOT. BUT WHAT WE'VE REALLY DONE IS CREATE A GHETTO THAT IS EASILY DISMISSED BY THE REST OF SOCIETY.
>
> – BOB BRINER, *ROARING LAMBS*

First, let me start with a disclaimer: I work both sides of the fence. As a commercial television producer, I'm one of three founders of a TV commercial company that produces premiere television spots, including a couple of Super Bowl commercials and a spot during the opening ceremonies of the 2008 Summer Olympics. I've produced programming for major networks including PBS and early in my career I would film anything that moved, including sports, TV specials, and more. But I've also been deeply involved in Christian media for more than 35 years. And it's that side of the fence – the Christian media – where my passion really lies.

My other company, Cooke Pictures, produces and consults with some of the largest media ministries in this country and around the world. We love what we do, and we love our clients. Our passion is about change – navigating the changing media universe for our clients and helping them create programming that connects with an audience.

We don't really consider ourselves a "Christian" production company. We're simply Christians who produce programming and create media. Our faith informs everything we do, and we want it to be organic within our projects. Jesus didn't give an explicitly religious message every time he encountered people; many times he wove it into a powerful story about the normal details of living.

If you've heard me speak or read my books or articles, you also know I'm a regular and vigorous critic of religious broadcasting. Not from an ivory tower perspective, where I have no skin in the game, I'm speaking out from the trenches. There are plenty of books – usually written by researchers and academics – that criticize various aspects of religious media, church marketing and branding. Some of those books are excellent, and some are quite terrible, but either way, they have nothing to lose because few of the writers have a vested interest in the industry.

But I do – I work in the industry that I'm critiquing. As a result, there is a raging conflict within me, and some of what I'll be discussing in this book represents that tension.

If you currently work in religious media, don't be offended – be challenged.

A few years ago a movie was released called "Galaxy Quest," starring Tim Allen and Sigourney Weaver. The movie website IMDB.com describes the comedy like this:

> Eighteen years after their sci-fi adventure show "Galaxy Quest" was canceled, actors Jason Nesmith, Gwen DeMarco, Alexander Dane, Tommy Webber, and Fred Kwan are making appearances at sci-fi conventions and store openings in costume and character. They're wallowing in despair and at each other's throats until aliens known as Thermians arrive and, having mistaken the show for fact and consequently modeling their entire culture around it, take them into space to save them from the genocidal General Sarris and his armada.

Galaxy Quest was obviously a satire on the Star Trek television and movie franchise. The plot, the characters, and the TV show – they were all one continuous joke on the classic creation by Gene Roddenberry. It was a terrific movie, and was loved by both Star Trek fans and critics alike.

The most fascinating aspect of the film was that while it was an outrageous satire and made great fun of the Star Trek franchise, it was also written and produced by people who obviously loved the original series. The inside jokes and outrageous parody worked so well because the creators loved Star Trek and that came through as you watched the film. *In an odd way, this book is my "Galaxy Quest" to the religious media.*

> **A TRUE RADICAL MUST BE A MAN OF ROOTS. IN WORDS THAT I HAVE USED ELSEWHERE, 'THE REVOLUTIONARY CAN BE AN "OUTSIDER" TO THE STRUCTURE HE WOULD SEE COLLAPSE: INDEED, HE MUST SET HIMSELF OUTSIDE OF IT. BUT THE RADICAL GOES TO THE ROOTS OF HIS OWN TRADITION. HE MUST LOVE IT: HE MUST WEEP OVER JERUSALEM, EVEN IF HE HAS TO PRONOUNCE ITS DOOM.**
> – JOHN A. T. ROBINSON, 20TH CENTURY NEW TESTAMENT SCHOLAR

I love the media and I love the church. The challenge is to reach the next generation – and the media will be a significant part of that effort. I know people are still debating the role of media and technology in the church and in evangelism, but as far as I'm concerned, we are already behind. For my money, it's time we moved past that tiring conversation and started working.

A few years ago, I spoke at the national media conference for a major Christian denomination. Afterwards I had lunch with the director of communications for the organization, and when I asked him about his most frustrating challenge, his reply was direct and surprising: "Drums," he said. "The debate over using drums in our worship services is so great, it might actually cause a schism in the entire organization."

I told him I thought we had crossed that bridge in the 1970s and 1980s. "Not in our denomination," he replied.

In a similar way, *The Boston Globe* recently reported on a local theological seminary who had received a major gift from a foundation to help them train students to use technology in the church. But the money couldn't be spent because there was a major hold-up – the seminary leadership hadn't decided if technology should even be used in the church.

Certainly churches and ministry organizations misuse the media and technology, and that's a significant part of this book, but it's time we moved past the debate and started making real change happen.

You're about to read some pretty harsh criticisms but only because I, more than many, know the power of what can be achieved by using media effectively. To be alive in America in the 21st century means living in, what I call, a "media-driven" culture.

With research that indicates we're being bombarded with advertising and marketing messages, with people consuming media at record levels, with web-based companies dominating global business, if we don't understand how to share our faith in the digital world, the church will continue its slide into irrelevance in the eyes of the culture.

Media matters, and if we're going to engage the greater culture that surrounds us today, simply sharing the gospel message inside the walls of the church isn't enough anymore. We simply have to have a voice in the media.

WHAT EXACTLY IS MEDIA?

In the new digital world, media has become culture. It's the experiences and information we consume everyday. Media is all of it: what we watch and listen to, the printed books, magazines, and advertisements we read, the news on cable, network TV, online, and print, and even the products, communications, and things we enjoy, need, and want on a daily basis.

It's the road the culture travels, and the way we connect.

Traditionally, people of faith have been highly engaged in the media of a particular time. From stone tablets to the Gutenberg printing press, for thousands of years, literacy has been driven by the need to know God and understand His purpose for our lives. Today is no different, and as I'll discuss throughout the book, we as Christians have been quite aggressive at sharing our faith through the media in the electronic age. However, while we started with good intentions, our execution has often been less than effective.

A BRIEF HISTORY OF RELIGIOUS MEDIA

I have been fascinated by the history of religious media for a long time. When it comes to movies for instance, the gap between film and faith for most Christians is wide and historic. But what most Christians fail to realize is that during the birth of the movie industry, the church was actually one of the largest producers of movies in America. In Terry Lindvall's fascinating book, *The Silents of God*, he takes the reader on a captivating journey through the early days of American cinema, when the imprint of the church was powerful and positive. Not only did Christians encourage movie attendance, but Christian organizations produced a massive number of films during the early part of this century.

Few people today know that Hollywood itself was actually built as a model Christian community. According to Lindvall, developer Horace Wilcot, a Bible believing real estate speculator, had a vision of creating a community with no saloons, no liquor, and free land for any Protestant church moving in.

If he could only see his dream today...

By 1900, the historic Tabernacle Church in Long Beach was designed as part sanctuary, part lecture hall and part theater. I visited a church in New Jersey that was built in 1911 and originally designed so the lobby could be used as a movie theater. The projection booth was built above the entrance, making it easy to project the movies on the lobby wall – in 1911.

As early as 1909, in a Nickelodeon magazine article entitled, *Minister Proposes Sunday Pictures*, the writer stated:

The Ithaca (New York) Journal says that a number of saloon-keepers of the city have been approached by one of Ithaca's ministers within the last few days and asked if they would contribute to the expense of putting on a moving pictures show at a local theater every Sunday evening to be followed by a short address. Illustrated songs are also intended to be a feature of the program.

It is the intention of the ministers to cooperate with the local law and order league and provide a place for men to go Sunday evenings, so that they will not be tempted or go to other towns for their amusement.

Other leaders agreed that movies and religion did indeed mix very well. In 1916, Edward McConoughey, wrote an article entitled, *Motion Pictures in Religious and Educational Work*:

Motion pictures have become one of the most important means for effective education. They have revolutionized the form in which narrative, drama, even the subject of religion itself is presented...The motion picture, therefore, should be an important part of the equipment of every religious and educational institution.

But it didn't take long for the divide to begin, and although some of the earliest motion pictures featured classic subjects such as the *Oberammergau Passion Play* (1898) and *The Temptation of St. Anthony* (1898), it wasn't long before the film industry and the Church were at odds with one another.

In that context, many Christians have historically believed that movies, if not sinful, at the very least did not reflect the abundant Christian life. Growing up, my family enjoyed watching movies, but there were plenty of folks in our church who felt that while movie attendance may not be an actual sin, should Jesus return while you were in the theater, all bets were off.

THE TEN COMMANDMENTS CONTROVERSY

Whenever I see Christians up in arms about the removal of monuments or statues honoring The Ten Commandments, I'm reminded that during the original production of the epic (and expensive) movie by Cecil B. DeMille, he executed an innovative and ingenious marketing stunt. As University of Florida professor James Twitchell, author of *Shopping For God* describes, DeMille partnered with the Fraternal Order of Eagles, a nationwide organization of civic clubs founded by movie theater owners, to sponsor the construction and placement of thousands of Ten Commandment monuments across the country. The idea was to link a religious notion to a promotional buzz about the upcoming movie, and hopefully drive audiences to the box office.

After all, since DeMille was Jewish, by building the monuments, he wasn't celebrating Christianity, he was promoting his movie.

Many years later, two of the DeMille inspired granite monuments – in Texas and Alabama – became such national controversies that the case for their removal went all the way to the U.S. Supreme Court. Thus, one of the biggest court cases regarding Christianity in the public square was essentially born of an entertainment-based promotional stunt.

THE CATHOLIC PERSPECTIVE

Looking back to the medieval period, the Catholic tradition has always embraced liturgy, music, drama, and pageantry. If you study the architecture of the great cathedrals of Europe, you'll find they were designed around an altar, where a wide variety of religious activities could take place. In fact, what we now call the medieval "miracle and mystery plays" that toured throughout Europe during this period were simply dramatic presentations that grew so popular and expansive they burst outside the walls of the church.

Based on Scripture, the plays and pageants recounted the great stories of the Bible, but soon, many wandered into telling tall tales that were neither remotely historic or biblical. In fact, my wife Kathleen and I had the opportunity to examine a few of the remaining original manuscripts of such plays that are archived in the British Museum in London. We were escorted by historian David Daniell, who wrote what many consider the definitive biography of William Tyndale, the man who translated the Bible into English. David was the curator of the Tyndale exhibition at the British museum and we interviewed him extensively for a film project about the translation of the Bible into English. His expertise on the manuscripts was remarkable.

David showed us that medieval play producers weren't that different from today's Hollywood producers. While their intentions were sound, ultimately, they were more interested in entertainment value than accuracy. While the stories *began* with scripture, they often veered in a different direction in order to tell more compelling and popular stories rather than being concerned with biblical scholarship. They were focused on making the ancient stories of the Bible come alive for their audience.

The Catholic tradition has always had a rich history of engagement with the culture through drama, music and art. Catholic leaders have always understood the power of compelling stories and their ability to reach into the hearts of the people.

Even from the perspective of architecture, the Church expressed a spiritual vision. For instance, Gothic architecture is not just a physical style, but rather a theological system that allows Christian principles to be expressed through design.

But by the time of the Protestant Reformation, a bridge had been crossed. In an understandable effort to reform theology based on the teachings of Martin Luther and his contemporaries, church leaders became a little too eager to discard some of the Catholic perspectives – particularly on the arts. The result had a powerful and extensively negative effect on culture both inside and outside of the church.

Particularly in countries where new "reformed" styles of worship became the rule, churches were often violently and crudely stripped of paintings, statues, and other religious ornamentation. If the artifacts could be burned, such as vestments, paintings, choir books, carved choir stalls, and other artistic expressions, they were added to the fire and if not, they were often painted over, whitewashed, or otherwise trashed.

Some of what survived destruction was only spared because doing so would have caused grave structural damage to the buildings themselves. As described by Peter and Linda Murray in *The Oxford Companion to Christian Art and Architecture*, between the Protestant Reformation and the French Revolution, the arts suffered through a long period of decline for which the Church is still trying to recover. Before the Reformation, churches were designed around an altar where liturgy, music, and drama flourished, but post-Reformation churches were transformed into auditoria, where the main emphasis became the pulpit.

In other words, churches that had previously been designed for the full expression of worship, including music, drama, and the arts, were now transformed into little more than an auditorium. It was a great advance for preaching and teaching, but other types of spiritual expression were easily discarded.

Manuscripts for plays were burned, musical compositions were lost, and paintings and statues were destroyed. It was indeed a dark time for the historic connection between the Church and the arts.

Since that time, the Church has been slow to reintroduce the dramatic arts and use them as tools for reaching a particular culture. A new generation, however, weaned on television, popular music, and films, has shown that drama can indeed be used by the Church to present a powerful witness to the eternal story of redemption, which is all about saving grace.

By comparison, common grace teaches that God can be found in the most unlikely of places – even the movies and other media. Catholic novelist Andrew Greeley effectively argues that God reveals Himself to us through the experiences, objects, and people we encounter in our lives. He states that "grace is everywhere." Certainly, we must be concerned for the poor but we must never forget the arts, for potentially, the artist is a sacrament maker – one who exposes and reveals the presence of God throughout creation.

A COMPLETELY RADICAL IDEA

When it comes to more contemporary media like radio and television, the story takes a different turn.

When Christians first began to embrace radio as early as 1921, and television around 1940, it wasn't the producers and directors that were the early adopters – it was the preachers.

Men like Paul Rader, Donald Grey Barnhouse, and William Ward Ayer pioneered radio for the church. Network radio powerhouses like *The Lutheran Hour* with Walter A. Maier and

The Old Fashioned Revival Hour with Charles E. Fuller had audiences in the millions. By 1942, Maier was receiving more mail than Amos 'n' Andy, and Fuller was the most popular program host on the Mutual Broadcasting Network. It's fair to say that in those days, the voice of Christians were some of the most popular and influential on national radio.

According to Mark Ward, Sr. in his book *The Air of Salvation*, it was Maier who actually preached the first non-denominational worship service featured on television. It was 1948, when he broadcast *The Lutheran Hour* locally over KSD-TV in St. Louis. During that time, a young evangelist named Oral Roberts was traveling the country with a custom-designed tent that could seat 10,000 people. At that time in America, the number of facilities that could accommodate a crowd of that size were few, so Oral and his technical team led by Collins Steele had to be inventive. With advice from Steele, his friend and associate, he designed a tent so large that it took multiple tractor-trailer rigs to carry the canvas, poles, and ropes, and based on sheer size, the caravan of an Oral Roberts Evangelistic campaign in those days must have looked pretty similar to the circus coming to town.

Honestly, few can imagine today what it would have been like in the 40s and 50s to see 10,000 people pouring into a tent in city after city across America. From a secular perspective, it would have been similar to the acclaim and influence of a rock star today. Not long after, a young pastor from Akron, Ohio named Rex Humbard suggested Oral begin filming his popular meetings for television.

It was a completely radical idea – but it made sense, so Oral packed his bags and headed west for a network introduction. A few years ago, Oral told me how nervous he was when he first visited the NBC network offices in Los Angeles in 1954. He told me that NBC welcomed him – especially considering the size of his audience, and lined him up with three national sponsors to pay for the program. But in those days, advertisers had a significant influence on the programs they sponsored, and in many cases exerted final approval over the content of the show, the producer, director, or cast.

Oral questioned that model – especially when those sponsors could potentially tell him how and what to preach – or at the very least, have editorial control over the finished program. After all, he was preaching the gospel, so how could he be influenced by a secular advertiser? After serious consideration, he reluctantly passed on the offer and traveled back to his hometown of Tulsa, Oklahoma to figure out an alternative approach.

AN IDEA THAT WOULD CHANGE EVERYTHING

Over the next few months, Oral had an idea that forever altered the relationship between Christians and the media. If a company that makes razor blades, soap, or hand cream could sponsor a program, why couldn't he? Why couldn't he just raise the money and buy the network time slot himself? And back to NBC he went.

It had never been done before, but according to Oral, NBC decided to give it a shot. In 1955, the *Abundant Life Program with Oral Roberts* debuted on selected NBC stations across America. I've seen the original films myself, and they did capture the raw, unplanned nature of Pentecostal evangelism back in those days. Beginning with that first program, Oral would remain on the air with very few breaks for more than forty years, generating massive national audiences at his peak in the 1970s. Oral even ventured into feature filmmaking with the production of a major dramatic movie called *Venture into Faith*, which told the story of a young boy's healing at – you guessed it – an Oral Roberts tent crusade. The movie was produced by Hollywood professionals, and by an incredible chance, early in my career I attended a film directing seminar and coincidentally, took a film class from Herb Lightman, the man who directed *Venture into Faith*. I still have an original poster of the movie in my office today.

Back in those days, when radio and television – and even movies – were embraced by Christians, it was usually the preachers like Oral Roberts and Billy Graham that jumped into the deep end first. They didn't really debate about the technology so much from a *theological* perspective, they just saw it as another opportunity for sharing the gospel. It was their vision for reaching mass audiences for evangelism that drove them to embrace radio and television with little hesitation. And for that, we have to give preachers of that era a huge amount of credit. They took the risk, and it's allowed the Christian message to reach literally hundreds of millions of people over the years.

While the positive side of the story is about preachers seizing the moment, the negative side of the story is about, well, preachers seizing the moment.

SERMON-DRIVEN MEDIA

For a preacher, the answer to every problem is a good sermon. Preaching is what they are called and trained to do, and it is the lens through which they view the world.

As a result, for the most part, religious radio and television have become sermon-driven media. Turn on religious radio or television today at random, and chances are you'll hear somebody preaching.

Is this a bad thing? Not necessarily. Having grown up as a preacher's kid, I still enjoy hearing a good sermon, and I'm a great advocate of religious teaching for religious audiences. In Los Angeles, on our local cable TV system we have about 500 channels, among which are what I would call *lifestyle specific channels*. We have multiple sports channels, cooking channels, music channels, home design channels, and gay and lesbian channels. There's a channel for every conceivable interest these days, to the point that I often joke about creating the "Trampoline Channel" – all trampoline, all the time.

SO WHY SHOULDN'T WE HAVE A CHRISTIAN CHANNEL?

The truth is, I don't find anything wrong with a TV channel for Christians who want to watch teaching, preaching and music just for them. I'm even prepared to defend what's right about religious media. True, as a Christian who is a producer and consultant in the media industry, I am often calling the religious media to a higher standard; but on the other hand, as a critic, it's easy to overlook the great things Christian media is accomplishing. That's why before we jump into the deep end of the pool, I should balance the scales a bit and look at what I consider to be some of the high points in Christian media:

Distribution

The truth is, it's tough to find a city or town in America that doesn't have a religious radio station, TV station or cable channel. The pioneers of Christian media were strong in the "business" of media, and today, the giants like Salem Communications, Trinity Broadcasting, Daystar, and others have covered the country with Christian broadcasting. Even overseas, God TV, HCJB Radio, the Far East Broadcasting Network, and others have taken a message of faith, literally, to the ends of the earth. The value of Christian broadcasting facilities and networks is in the billions of dollars, and the global reach is significant. Regardless of what you think of the programming or theology of specific networks and programmers, it is hard to deny that these organizations have grown to international proportions, and are truly significant players from a business perspective.

Likewise, religious recording and publishing have grown to major magnitude as well. Some have become so popular they've been acquired by successful secular publishing houses and record labels. If their acquisition by secular companies has been a positive or negative issue is another book, but there's no question that religious media – specifically Christian media – now reaches vast global audiences.

Quality
While there are certainly far too many churches, ministries, and stations using out-of-date equipment, with facilities that are in bad shape, the major media organizations and ministries have made a real commitment to quality. Today, many major religious networks as well as local churches are completely digital. Many local radio stations can boast state-of-the-art studios and facilities.

I'm proud to say that Cooke Pictures has been a part of this movement, helping churches and ministry organizations move into the High Definition world. HD is the standard format for a growing number of religious media organizations. Today – especially with advancing technology and lowering prices – even small churches and ministries have begun to understand that quality technology can broaden your reach and impact.

Visual Liturgy
Churches are realizing the power of using video as a companion to worship. A new generation of innovators is helping pastors understand how to incorporate powerful images and graphics into the worship experience. You don't have to search long on the web to find a multitude of resources to help churches use visual media more expressively. And I'm not just talking about pictures of crosses on video screens or lyrics printed over nature scenes. Churches are using short films, music videos, scenes from mainstream movies, and other sophisticated media to enhance the worship and teaching experience.

Education
The first Christian media workshop I attended more than 20 years ago featured a TV station owner teaching us how to persuade

our brother-in-law to help us build studio sets for free. I walked
out. But today, the National Religious Broadcasters, The Reach
Conference, Biola Media Conference, Technologies for Worship,
Compass Academy, Echo, and others are training a new generation of Christian communicators. I've lectured on the subject of
religious media at major universities including the University of
California at Berkeley, and UCLA. As I write this chapter I just
returned from speaking at Yale University for a symposium on
how religious media is impacting the world. There is a hunger
for this content and it is being addressed, in an increasingly
sophisticated way.

Media Savvy Pastors

As I mentioned before, while an earlier generation of pastors
and ministry leaders pioneered radio and TV, most of them
didn't really understand how to use it effectively. They were
often great preachers, but were limited by their lack of knowledge of the media itself. But today, new generations of pastors
and ministry leaders have embraced the media, and are pushing the boundaries of what it can accomplish. Rather than create another typical religious television program, Pastor Erwin
Rafael McManus created "Crave" – a series of short films based
on his bestselling book, *Soul Cravings*. The project has been distributed – not by a religious media outlet, but a major Hollywood film studio. Pastor Mark Crow in Oklahoma City created
an online TV network at vc.tv. Joel Osteen's podcast is one of
the most popular downloads on Apple's iTunes platform. More
and more pastors and ministry leaders are breaking out of the
box of traditional media, and as a result, reaching a new (and
younger) audience.

Independent Producers

While some of the major networks are making change happen
on a limited scale, most of the flood of change in the industry has
been at the hands of independent, faith-driven producers. With

limited funding, and inadequate resources, a new generation of producers is moving in new directions with short films, feature documentaries, interactive DVD's, branded content, and other integrated media. For instance, they recognize that a significant platform for tomorrow's TV will be the cell phone, and to reach the next generation, we have to penetrate at that level. The next instrumental Christian media pioneer is probably working away right now on a computer in his or her dad's garage.

THE CHRISTIAN MEDIA BUBBLE

So there are plenty of good things happening in religious media, and for those seeking religious instruction, compelling preaching, children's programming and more, Christian broadcasters and programmers are improving. Through it's wide availability the existing religious media is making an impact. At the same time, I have a problem with people who live 24/7 in what I call the "Christian Bubble." By Christian Bubble, I simply mean people who live so deep inside the influence of Christian radio, publishing, TV, or music that they have no other perspective. For an earlier generation, people of faith actually interacted with the culture around them, but 30 to 40 years ago, it was discovered that the Christian audience was a *buying* audience, at which point, *we stopped preaching to the world, and started preaching to each other*. As a result, entire industries were built around "Christian" radio, television, publishing, or recording.

Is this a bad thing? Not necessarily. The problem is not really with the media itself but rather how it is consumed. The problem occurs when Christian media becomes one's only source of influence. I have friends who only buy Christian music, watch Christian TV, or listen to Christian radio. They'd rather watch a poorly produced, mediocre *Christian* movie than an excellent, well-made *secular* film.

So what's the problem? People are free to enjoy whatever they want, right? The problem with living "in the bubble" is that we stop doing what Jesus called us to do. The Great Commission is about going into all the world, not just the safe and insulated world that exists within Christian media.

> THE BIG MONEY IS NOT AT THE BOX OFFICE GROSS BUT IN THE, SAY, TEN MILLION DVD'S THAT COME AFTER THE SHOW. PEOPLE WANT TO OWN THIS "TEXT," AND ADD IT TO THEIR VIDEO "LIBRARY." IN EARLIER DAYS, A FAMILY HAD A GOING-TO-CHURCH BIBLE AND A STAY-AT-HOME FAMILY BIBLE. THE FAMILY BIBLE NOW SITS NEXT TO "THE PASSION" DVD.
>
> – JAMES B. TWICHELL, *SHOPPING FOR GOD*

THE PARADOX OF "SAFE" MEDIA

At the risk of generating some hate mail, I'm going to put this out there: I'm particularly uncomfortable with "safe" media. "Family safe" is something you hear a lot on Christian radio and TV. But try as I might, I just can't find anything in the Bible that calls us to live "safe" lives. It wasn't very safe for Jesus to say the things he did. People who have boldly preached the gospel throughout history have been beaten, tortured, and burned at the stake – so why would I expect the media expressing that story to me and my family to be safe?

I understand that there is real reason for caution when we consider much of the values, including gratuitous sexuality, violence, and profanity on network television. As a young starlet named Marilyn Monroe once said, "Hollywood is a place where they'll pay you $10,000 for a kiss and fifty cents for your soul." So with that in mind, here are a few ideas to consider:

First, it's about balance.
Remember, I work in Christian media, so I'm not talking about dumping all religious radio and TV, but I am advocating for

the occasional breath of fresh air. Full-time immersion in *anything* can screw up your perspective about life. Jesus was concerned about fishing, weddings and building tables and chairs. His friends and disciples weren't religious leaders, they were a fascinating cross-section of the culture of the time. Avoiding interaction with the culture wasn't an option for the early church, and it shouldn't be for us either.

Second, protect the kids.

Don't do it by saying "no" or shutting off the outside world. *Take the time to teach your kids about life.* Watch TV with them, see movies together, and help them discover how to navigate their place as a Christian in the culture. Believe me, if you tell them no, chances are, they'll watch it at a friend's house. My wife Kathleen and I raised our two daughters during a time when sex, violence, and profanity skyrocketed in television and movies. Music videos were not exactly "cultural treasures."

As traditional notions of the family were taking a beating in the media, we didn't shelter them – we walked them through it. If they really wanted to see a movie, television program, or concert that we thought was morally questionable, we would go with them, and discuss the choices the characters or performers made, and why they made them. I still remember those "after the movie talks" as some of the most memorable times we spent with Kelsey and Bailey. As a result, today they have a vocabulary with which to encounter the culture and the media. Plus – because we didn't actively keep them away from many of these movies and television programs, or make a big deal about it, they often lost interest. We didn't make it more desirable by restricting it.

Now I don't want to give the impression that we let them watch anything. We did have restrictions, but because we allowed them wide latitude and talked to them frankly about our reasons, they rarely questioned us when we drew a line in the sand.

Third, understand that culture happens.

We're never going to be "family safe" – especially if you're committed to sharing God's message of hope with the world. Just ask the house church pastors in China, or Christian leaders in the Sudan. Following Jesus is costly and involves a risk. Frederica Mathewes-Green criticizes Christians who constantly talk about "changing the culture." As she wrote in *Christianity Today* magazine:

> The culture, then, is like the weather. We may be able to influence it in modest ways, like seeding the clouds, but it is a recipe for frustration to expect that we can direct it. Nor should we expect positive change without some simultaneous downturn in a different corner. Nor should we expect that any change will be permanent. The culture will always be shifting, and it will always be with us.
>
> God has not called us to change the weather. Our primary task as believers, and our best hope for lasting success, is to care for individuals caught up in the pounding storm. They are trying to make sense of their lives with inadequate resources, confused and misled by the Evil One and unable to tell their left hand from their right (Jonah 4:11). They are not a united force; they are not even in solidarity with each other, apart from the unhappy solidarity of being molded by the same junk-food entertainment. They are sheep without a shepherd, harassed and helpless (Matt. 9:36). Only from a spot of grounded safety can anyone discern what to approve and what to reject in the common culture.
>
> Culture is not a monolithic power we must defeat. It is the battering weather conditions that people, harassed and helpless, endure. We are sent out into the storm like a St. Bernard with a keg around our neck, to comfort, reach, and rescue those who are thirsting, most of all, for Jesus Christ.

Fourth, we're not "taking America back."
We're not going back to the picket fence era of the 1950s and I'm sure quite a few African-American believers and working women are fine with that. The culture is moving forward, and we need to do the same. Media ministries have wasted far too much money in fundraising campaigns focused on returning America to some idyllic state, rather than dealing with the America that exists today.

The disciples may have dreamed about going back to a day when Israel was a free nation, but they also knew that they had to act based on the reality of the moment, which was Roman occupation.

Finally, popping the bubble will deepen your own faith.
Listen to a little rock and roll, opera, or jazz, go to an art museum, read a good classic novel, go see an action movie or a love story. Remember the concept of *common grace* and start looking for God in the most unlikely places. You'll be shocked to find that Jesus shows up in places we wouldn't normally think are very "Christian."

Jesus spent his time where the people were – in the marketplace, social gatherings, on the road, and in the homes of friends.

So what are we doing in a bubble?

> **COMMUNICATION DOES NOT BEGIN WITH WORDS; IT
> BEGINS WITH CONNECTION.**
> — JEDD MEDEFIND & ERIK LOKKESMOE,
> *THE REVOLUTIONARY COMMUNICATOR*

I was in a strategic planning meeting with a major media ministry recently – an organization that's done a lot of good in the world, but which currently operates under two great myths:

1) We need more research before we can make a decision.
2) The older audience still supports what we do.

To a degree, both are true for many, if not most traditional media ministries today, but taken to extremes, they are stifling, burdensome and crushing blows that keep organizations from achieving real growth.

THE MYTH: WE NEED MORE RESEARCH

For most of my career, I've called for more research on the audience that listens to and watches religious media. After all, how are we going to know what they're interested in if we don't know who they are? Mainstream media spends millions on audience research, trying to find links to buying habits, emotional connections, viewing preferences, demographic information, and more. I've conducted focus groups where we gather different types of people in a room, show them TV programs, movie clips, or commercials, and discuss what they liked and didn't like – all in an effort to extrapolate more insight for future programming ideas.

In spite of tens of millions of dollars spent on audience research, the major TV networks still produce clunkers every season. Research can't provide all the answers, and at some point, we simply have to act from experience, expertise and sometimes, our gut. After all, if it was easy, everyone would be successful.

As I did the final edit on this chapter, the Los Angeles Times reported that the top three programming executives for NBC were purged, signaling real desperation at the network. In spite of hundreds of millions invested in top talent, audience research, programming expertise, and advertising, during the fall of 2008, NBC slid to fourth in the network ratings. Indeed, all the research in the world can't predict the fickle nature of TV audiences.

The illusive pursuit of audience intelligence will continue until we can somehow tap directly into their cortex and discover what they're thinking and feeling. (No doubt network research departments are experimenting with that right now.)

THE TRUTH IS MORE IMPORTANT THAN THE FACTS.

– FRANK LLOYD WRIGHT

It's worth mentioning that traditional research such as focus groups, paper surveys, phone interviews and more are not just expensive, but often unnecessary. Today, I'm finding that direct mail questionnaires, e-mail surveys, online evaluations, and customer chat are less expensive options worth considering. Plus, if you're listening, you'll be amazed at the information on you can glean from blogs, message boards, web forums, online polls, chat rooms, and even YouTube.

But no matter what your strategy, at some point – right or wrong - you have to take a shot. In most cases with religious and non-profit media organizations, we simply don't have the money for adequate research, or at best, there is limited funding even for partial studies. Either way, at some point, we need to make strategic decisions with the information we have and take action.

Most management experts agree that you can't keep waiting forever for the next study. If you have 65-70 percent of the research or data completed, then it's time to make a decision. Insecure leaders are hesitant to stick their necks out; they know that research gives them an easy source of blame should the project go badly.

But in the digital media world, waiting for more data can be deadly. Sure we'd like to know more and more about the viewing or listening habits of the audience, but those habits are changing dramatically as technology changes. Today, far too many churches and ministries are paralyzed because they feel *if they could just get their hands on one more report or hear from one more expert*, they'd have the answers they need to make a decision.

The bottom line is that information is great when you have it, but don't be paralyzed when it doesn't exist.

THE MEDIA REVOLUTION ISN'T FOR SISSIES

The media revolution is for people with the courage of their convictions, and who can make bold decisions – with or without confirming research. So don't live in fear – afraid to make a decision because it might be wrong.

Trust me – most of your decisions will be wrong.

During any time of transition, only the bold survive. This isn't a time for placing blame, finding scapegoats, or looking for a fall guy. It's dangerous new territory, and to influence the next generation will take enormous courage, conviction, and determination. It will also take a positive approach to your team. When serious cultural change happens, failure will be more common than success. In such an environment, *you should reward innovation, not just success.* Certainly everyone wants to succeed, but during times of change, success is rare. Thomas Edison said, "I have not failed. I've just found 10,000 ways that won't work." It was that kind of attitude that created the light bulb and hundreds of other inventions that dramatically changed modern life.

If you manage your people by fear of failure, then failure is exactly what you'll achieve.

THE MYTH: THE OLDER AUDIENCE STILL SUPPORTS WHAT WE'RE DOING

This is especially damaging because it's *partly true.* I remember when I was going through the agony of my Ph.D. work, we discussed a principle in theology that the most damaging heresies are the ones that actually make sense. It's easy to dismiss obvious errors because they just don't add up, but there are plenty of Christian leaders teaching error because there's enough truth in it to make the concept sound viable. I'm reminded of that principle when clients tell us that they must be doing something right, because they're still receiving support from the older audience.

It's true. There is still an audience that remembers the peak of traditional Christian broadcasting and probably supported men like Billy Graham, Oral Roberts, Paul Crouch, Pat Robertson, D. James Kennedy and Jerry Falwell. And those folks are still out there, faithfully supporting ministries as they have for years. They are wonderful people who captured the initial vision of religious broadcasting and all its potential.

The problem is that picture is really a mirage – like a waving unreal image in the steaming desert. These wonderful people are supporting you now, but in a relatively short while, they will be gone – replaced by another generation who doesn't have that same vision and commitment.

Some of you will argue that older people just naturally gravitate to religion as they age, and as such, you will always have a support base, but there's a serious error in this type of thinking.

IT'S NOT ABOUT *AGE*, IT'S ABOUT *HOW PEOPLE COMMUNICATE*

What's left of the current generation of seniors (I'm mostly talking about the boomers' parents) communicate primarily through snail mail and the telephone. This is the audience that drives TV telethons, and responds most quickly to direct mail campaigns. They are eager to pick up the phone and pledge to a television program.

As I write this book, this older audience is the backbone of most media ministries today. As a result, the major radio and TV ministries are built around direct mail. While there are certain variations to the model, the basic concept is that TV and radio are impulse media – they get the listener or viewer to make an emotional response to a donor appeal by picking up the phone and calling, or sending in a letter. From that point, a direct mail campaign kicks-in to develop and nurture a relationship with the donor. From a fundraising perspective, radio and TV act as a net to acquire names, and those names are developed into donors through a monthly direct mail program.

And believe me, direct mail is critical. I remember the early days before direct deposit, when it was absolutely essential to make sure a ministry letter arrived on the first of the month when the donor had just deposited their payroll check and the bank account was full. I've actually seen direct mail companies fired by organizations because they couldn't get the "drop date" right for the letters. It was science as much as ministry in those days – and in other ways, it still is today.

Now, in the age of direct deposit, the drop date isn't so critical, but there are a host of other issues at stake when it comes to fundraising for ministry. Is this a criticism? Absolutely not. Of course there are unscrupulous organizations out there, and more than a few I'd like to see shut down completely. But the vast majority of churches and ministries – and the fundraising consultants they employ – are godly men and women, who agonize over the most effective way to raise the funds necessary to make ministry thrive.

My experience indicates that if Christians simply gave 10 percent of their income most, if not all, ministry work on the planet would be funded. Sadly – especially in the richest country in the world – most believers today give at shamefully low levels.

But the older generation who still give – the core group of donors of most major ministries – are dwindling. Most organizations I work with would echo the fact that among the older age group, their lists are getting smaller every year.

It's not the dwindling number of older donors that worries me – it's the change in the way they communicate.

There will always be an older generation; and my generation – the baby boomers – will probably be the biggest and baddest of them all. Our generation has determined buying trends for most of our lives, and we don't plan to stop now. From the time we all wore Roy Rogers six-shooters to our Rolex or Brietling watches today, we have had a powerful and lasting impact on the culture.

But we don't communicate the way our parents did.

I don't know about you, but I've never once picked up the phone or written a letter to make a donation. I'm more likely to donate via the web or use automatic funds transfer from the bank. The hassle of writing a check every month or talking to a college kid at some call center has no interest for me. Churches, ministries, and non-profits – are you listening?

Every generation communicates in a different way. It is no longer how we want to communicate with donors but rather how they want to communicate with us. And if we're not ready, they'll take their money elsewhere.

So don't buy into the myth that everything is OK because the old folks are still giving you money. One ministry TV producer said it this way: *"Back in the late seventies we could turn our cameras to the audience and they were all seniors. Now, thirty years later I can do they same and they're still seniors. Different people, but the same age group."*

His point was that their ministry should continue doing the same thing in the same way because they're still appealing to the same older demographic group. What he doesn't realize is that I'm not changing my way of communicating when I become a senior citizen. I will age, but I still want my mobile phone, my laptop, my email, my instant messaging, my social networks, all my technology – *and* my Brietling watch.

Even more important for our subject – the way I communicate with non-profits, churches, and ministries (and the ones I choose to communicate with) will be dramatically different from the habits of my parents.

THE NEED FOR BRUTAL HONESTY

THE WEIGHT OF THIS SAD TIME WE MUST OBEY.
SPEAK WHAT WE FEEL, NOT WHAT WE OUGHT TO SAY.
– EDGAR FROM SHAKESPEARE'S *KING LEAR*

Perhaps what Christian media needs is a little brutal honesty. I had an interesting experience recently when talking to the marketing director at a major American church denomination. His organization is going through a difficult transition, has some financial challenges, and the future is uncertain. Especially from a communications and branding perspective, they need real help. So the marketing director went to the leader of the organization and suggested they bring my team in to explore the possibilities. The leader knew me personally and said that he really liked what Cooke Pictures had accomplished with other organizations; he agreed that we were excellent in these situations. Regardless, he did not invite us in for a meeting. When asked why not, the leader responded, "Because Phil is brutally honest, and I don't think we're ready for that."

When this story was relayed to me, I stopped in my tracks for a moment. I know that I do have a reputation for being honest and frank, (after all, I'm writing this book) but I had not considered it would be a reputation that would cost us clients. I began some soul searching about how to speak the truth – in love of course – but speak the truth nevertheless.

> **MEN OCCASIONALLY STUMBLE OVER THE TRUTH, BUT MOST OF THEM PICK THEMSELVES UP AND HURRY OFF AS IF NOTHING HAD HAPPENED.**
> – WINSTON CHURCHILL

There are plenty of Christians – including consultants and media people – that sugarcoat issues. They are more concerned with keeping the business or staying employed than risking it all on speaking truth into a situation. And in the spirit of full-disclosure, I too have wrestled with the decision to tell the whole, hard truth.

I was recently reminded of Randy Pausch, a Carnegie-Mellon professor, who delivered his now famous "Last Lecture" while terminally ill with pancreatic cancer. His last lecture to his students was based on his principles for living, and it's been seen so often on YouTube, that a book was eventually published. One of the principles he discussed with his students was simple:

> If I could leave you with only 3 words, those words would be TELL THE TRUTH. If I could leave you with 3 more, it would be ALL THE TIME.

TELL THE TRUTH, ALL THE TIME

I am not implying that all Christians are liars, but I've discovered that we often become so concerned with everyone's *feelings*, that we've forgotten how to speak the *truth*. How many failed ministry projects, bad media programs, screwed up organizations, insecure leaders – not to mention millions of wasted donor dollars - could have been saved had someone at a critical moment had the courage to speak the truth?

Obviously telling the truth needs to be done for the right reasons, in love, with respect, and through appropriate channels. But it needs to be done. In the church today, we even have a skewed perception of judgment. The mistaken attitude that we have no business judging other believers is so pervasive – especially in the Charismatic and Pentecostal wing of the church – that I think it's time to reconsider what "judgment" really means. The scripture from Matthew 7:1, "Do not judge," has been so misunderstood – particularly as it relates to Christians in the media – I think we need to reexamine judgment and what it means.

DID JESUS REALLY MEAN THAT WE SHOULD NEVER JUDGE OTHERS?

It's interesting that when you examine the Scriptures related to judgment, it's not just the act of judging that Jesus is talking about as much as *our attitude while doing it*. After all, common sense tells us that making judgments is important and we're required to do it on a daily basis. Good judgment is a part of life – who we let our children play with, what church to attend, where we work, who we associate with and how we spend our time are all judgments.

In a fallen and sinful world, people must be held account-able. Today the culture tries to convince us that tolerance is the highest virtue. *Who are you to judge?* is the rallying cry of devi-ant behavior, heretical teaching and immoral living. There's nothing the enemy would love more than if we as believers gave up calling sinners to repentance. What would our society become if we stopped evaluating student performance, keep-ing leaders accountable or arresting criminals? Judgment is unavoidable; good judgment is invaluable.

Without proper criticism and judgment, living in real community would become impossible. Not only do we have to judge, but we are called to judge, and in today's society, we need to be more vigilant than ever about judgment.

The question becomes, how do we judge like Jesus would, and how can we be sure that love, repentance, and restora-tion are the principles we put first when making decisions? Anyone can have an opinion, but true judgment happens only after serious examination, reflection, and consultation with Scripture.

We can't be frivolous, especially when dealing with an alleged sin of a pastor or Christian leader, but if we follow Scripture and investigate properly, we can arrive at a proper decision. Paul's writings to Timothy and the church in Corinth are virtual manuals about judgment and correction within the context of the Church.

LOSE THE BEAM

When Jesus taught about judgement in Matthew 7:3-5, he was speaking in the context of a hypercritical religious system that said one thing and did another. The Pharisees couldn't see clearly because of their own sin, and yet felt perfectly free to judge and condemn others. Nowhere in the Bible does it say we have to be absolutely perfect in word and deed before we can practice discernment, but if we point the finger at someone else, we need to be living right before God and have a clean conscience. If you look at the entire passage in context, it doesn't tell us not to judge – it tells us to withhold judgment until we can remove the beam in our own eye – at which point we may be able to see clearly. In other words, don't be a hypocrite.

JUDGING ACTIONS AND JUDGING PEOPLE ARE DRAMATICALLY DIFFERENT ISSUES

There's never a place for gossip, strife, or personal attacks in the Church, but serious discernment on issues of doctrine, performance, quality, professionalism, stewardship, skill, and results are absolutely necessary. We can love a pastor or leader, but when their lifestyle becomes abusive or their teaching aberrant, it's critical for the life of the Church that they be held accountable. Likewise, when a Christian employee does a poor job at work, they need to be disciplined. It's not about them personally, it's about their performance and the impact it's having on others.

This may be my single greatest issue with the hesitation to judge today. Evaluating a person is a grave and serious matter. However, it's of utmost importance that we judge the quality of our work, whether it be our teaching ability, people skills or preaching. Whatever our work, it should be evaluated. If we're ever going to raise the bar and build ministries that are more effective, we need the ability to evaluate the quality and worth of the work we do. When God spoke to Solomon to build his temple, he didn't hire good-hearted losers. He hired the best craftsmen and artists in the land.

Someone had to judge who the best craftsmen and artists were.

The gospel deserves no less than excellence, or at the very least, I believe we're called to reach as high as we can with the talent and resources we are given. Pastor and writer Erwin McManus calls that kind of effort "raw beauty." Just as Olympic judges determine the excellence of athletes, we need to call believers to authenticity and excellence in the Christian community. A hopeful Christian movie producer may have all the right intentions and motives in producing a movie, but if his skill is lacking, and the film is poorly made, what does that say to the culture about our stewardship of finances, or the botched presentation of the gospel? Are we happy to sit back and watch other Christians damage our witness to the culture by producing lousy movies, or should we lovingly call them to a higher standard?

EXECUTION MATTERS

When I say "execution" I'm not talking about killing people. Recently, a major movie critic reviewed a new Christian film that he called, "…*sadly and typically, another badly produced, over-acted, syrupy, spiritually themed movie.*" The reviewer had no problem with the Christian content – just the execution. That's the way the world looks at Christian work, because we've refused to hold Christian producers to a higher standard of quality.

Recently, I met a member of a mega-church in the South where the pastor divorced his wife, but never missed a day in the pulpit. The member defended the pastor comparing him to King David, who he pointed out had sinned, but was forgiven by God, without having to step down as King. I reminded him that David was the *political* leader of his time, not the *spiritual* leader. The pastor, in this instance, could be better compared to Samuel – Israel's spiritual leader – and the Scriptures require that we hold spiritual leaders to a higher level of accountability and responsibility. (I also encouraged him to read a little further and see the staggering consequences of David's sin.)

Despite the salvation experience, we are all still fallen creatures. Without discipline and work, often our natural tendency is to take the easy way out. Today, regardless of the intentions of their leaders, many churches and ministries fall short, hurting the Christian witness around the world, and damaging our credibility in the culture. As a Church, we need to rise up, stop our giving, write letters, and call these leaders into account.

The truth is, the Church today has it backwards. We spend too much time criticizing the outside culture, and not enough time holding each other to a higher standard.

Paul wrote in 1 Corinthians 5:13, *"God will judge those outside. Expel the wicked man from among you."* And yet today, churches and ministries raise millions to boycott and protest network television, secular movies, and mainstream culture, and all the while, we're dropping the ball when it comes to keeping our own house in order. When the world sees Christians using political influence to do something they view as trivial – like fighting for the right to say a prayer before a high school football game – while simultaneously watching Christian leaders flaunt morality, they have little reason to switch sides in the debate.

That's why if we can't have a conversation within the church about religious movies that fail, books that miss the mark, ministries that are ineffective, or pastors who fall short, our future will likely be a long slide into oblivion. However, if we can humble ourselves, pray that God gives us discernment, and always keep the goal of correction and restoration in mind, then we should feel empowered to seek the truth in all things.

It never hurts to keep in mind that our ability to judge is always limited, and one day, we'll all stand on level ground before the ultimate Judge.

Until that time, I hope we can overcome the fear, and continue calling each other to task for our many failures and shortcomings, so that we can, as Paul said, *"…press on toward the goal to win the prize for which God has called me heavenward in Christ Jesus."*

Perhaps the best compliment about my book *Branding Faith* came from Walden Media consultant John Seel when he honestly told me, "I originally bought the book to refute it. I thought it was just another one-sided promotion of church marketing, and I was prepared to argue against it. But once I read it, I discovered it was most discerning book about marketing and branding I'd ever read." He meant that rather than going full bore toward or against church and ministry marketing, it was an exploration of both possibilities and a balanced discussion of both sides. From a marketing consultant for movies like "The Chronicles of Narnia" that's pretty high praise.

If you speak the truth into your church, ministry, nonprofit, personal relationships, business – wherever – and you do it with grace, compassion, and discernment, whether or not it is accepted or rejected is not your problem. You've done your job. Be discerning and be gracious, but speak the truth - all the time.

And that's exactly what we're about to do…

CHAPTER THREE
THE WACKY FACTOR

I grew up as a preacher's kid in the South. As a result, I've been involved behind the scenes at churches and ministry organizations all of my life. I often tell people I came to faith in Christ "through the stage door."

But that unique perspective has made me wonderfully sensitive to the pitfalls of trying to use extremes in evangelism. As a kid I saw pastors shave their heads or get dunked in water if we brought enough kids to Sunday school. I've seen others sit in chairs atop high poles until attendance reached a certain number.

Don't get me wrong, some outrageous stunts are done in lighthearted fun, but others reap very unexpected and often disastrous results, especially when it comes to the issue of perception within the culture.

As I write this chapter, I've just finished watching a video clip from the "Divorce Court" TV show, promoting the appearance of evangelist Juanita Bynum to discuss her high profile divorce from her former husband, Bishop Thomas Weeks. She also appears to be giving advice to another guest – would you call her a "contestant?" I'm not actually sure about that one.

I'm also not sure where along the line divorced pastors started using TV programs like "Divorce Court" for publicity, but even for a grizzled religious media veteran like me, it was a surprise.

The *Atlanta Journal Constitution* wondered if the TV appearance was a ploy to extend her stay in the limelight, and I would have to agree after seeing the avalanche of charges, counter charges, newspaper coverage, and even YouTube videos on the issue. Before "Divorce Court," Juanita took her case against her husband the bishop to the public on YouTube, so her efforts to get her story told are prodigious.

And as a side rant, I've often wondered why those who have been through a divorce feel compelled to advise others about marriage. I have the greatest respect and compassion for anyone who's experienced the devastating impact of a failed marriage; but I wouldn't consult those who flunked their driver's exam on how to pass the DMV test. I think I'd rather seek the advice of those who have mastered the challenge.

I have serious doubts that non-believers will hold a higher view of either marriage or Christianity after seeing a celebrity pastor on an episode of "Divorce Court."

Through the years, there have been plenty of examples of Christians who simply look wacky to the non-believing culture – even when they might be well meaning. Decades ago, I met a member of a fairly large group that met at a Los Angeles bar every Sunday to make fun of Ernest Angsley's weekly religious TV program.

When Oral Roberts attempted to raise the remaining $8 million to build the City of Faith hospital years ago, he said that he really felt God telling him that this was his last great project. He had already built a major Christian university, and was now getting older, and knew this would be his last significant achievement. As a result, Oral felt a real urgency to move the hospital project forward. Without understanding the nuances of public relations, Oral went on his national television program and explained how he felt, directly to his TV viewers. The result was the press misunderstanding that if he didn't raise enough money, *God was going to kill him.*

No matter how you feel about Oral's sincerity regarding the project, his inability to express his feelings appropriately to the national media literally destroyed the project's potential. The resulting public relations snafu crippled future fundraising to the point that the City of Faith was eventually closed down and today the buildings are leased as office space.   While no one factor can determine the success or failure of a project of that magnitude, there's no question that the public's poor perception of that particular fundraising incident helped kill the project. As a result, the noble vision of creating a major medical center uniting faith and medicine was never realized.

GOOD PEOPLE TRYING TO DO THE RIGHT THING CAN STILL GET IT WRONG

In a local church we raise our hands in worship, encourage altar calls, participate in communion, or pray for the sick. Some folks get happy and like to clap or dance in worship. Christians do plenty of things that seem absolutely normal in a local, worshipping community – but show some of these same activities on television and we simply look nuts.

I recently watched a Christian TV network's national coverage of a major Pentecostal conference. At one point in the worship service, everyone literally fell on their face to God in prayer. While I don't question the authenticity of that moment, I do wonder if running nearly 20 minutes of a national TV program with no one speaking or singing, and nothing but a crane camera shot moving back and forth over an empty stage with 5 or 6 people laying prostrate on the stage was effective programming.

What would non-believers think if they had tuned in during those 20 minutes?

Defenders might respond that non-believing viewers of the event would surely feel the presence of the Holy Spirit. But *I* didn't feel it, and I'm a Christian. I just felt acute embarrassment. I think capturing that moment is fine – but having someone on camera explaining what was happening could have communicated a lot to both believers and non-believers.

God does remarkable things in the lives of believers, but to a non-believing audience it can appear crazy. Even Peter felt the need to explain what happened when the Holy Spirit descended on the believers in Jerusalem. "These are not drunken as you suppose" was a fantastic opening line that allowed him to preach to the unbelievers in the crowd. As a result, many were brought to faith from an event which – without proper explanation – they would have never understood.

And not only would they have never understood it, they would have labeled the early church as completely nuts.

NOT EVERYTHING WORKS ON TELEVISION

You've no doubt seen national news coverage of "church scenes" during coverage of politics, local government, or a social cause. They will sometimes highlight scenes from a local worship service, and I'm invariably uncomfortable seeing the worshippers and their service in the context of the evening news. What would appear completely normal in the service, somehow looks out of place, abnormal, or weird in the context of a political story on TV.

We often attribute the awkwardness of those moments to the bias of the reporter, but it's really about the bias of the medium.

At this point, I always have someone protest that I'm trying to compromise the gospel message by limiting what we can do on television. No, I'm simply trying to pave the way, so more people will *hear* the message.

How you present your message, and the medium you present it through has a significant impact on how that message is received.

Does your gold furniture, bad hair, excessive plants on stage, poor lighting or overdone makeup turn people away before they ever hear your message? Likewise, does the style of your service or the way you preach limit your audience? In other words, is preaching your message any way you choose worth driving people away from the gospel?

Part of the resistance of this generation to Christian media has been the wacky factor. Young people today look at religious media and it just seems so out of touch with the rest of their lives. From tacky sets and quaint accents to outdated styles and over-the-top emotions, there's a significant disconnect between the Christian media and what they experience everywhere else. Just listen to many family-oriented Christian radio programs, and you'll hear discussions that often seem remarkably out of touch and unrealistic. Parents today are caught in the real world, and need real world advice. I heard a movie review from a Christian program, where the reviewer cautioned about "upper male nudity" because a *male* character in the film took his shirt off during a pick-up basketball game.

Sheesh.

Yes, people turn away from the gospel. The rich young ruler walked away from Jesus. But just as with the rich young ruler, it would be better if the disconnect was because he couldn't handle the *message*. Too often in religious media, the disconnect comes from well meaning but out of touch people whose inability to communicate creates an obstacle that's impossible for the audience to overcome. They never even get to the message.

It's not about compromising our message, it's about respecting the audience enough to speak in a language and style they understand.

The gospel filters people. Just like the parable of the seed sown on different types of soil, some people welcome the good news, others believe but eventually wander away, while some run away immediately.

No matter what happens, the *content* of the gospel should be the filter, not our poor or inept *presentation* of that content. It is a sad day when someone turns away because of *us*.

OUR ATTITUDE TOWARD CULTURE

One of our greatest hindrances in changing the culture is our tendency as Christians to over-intellectualize everything. While I believe in intellectual excellence, there also comes a time when we need to actually *pull the trigger on the starting gun*. I often think that if I have to attend one more Christian conference where we all sit around talking about the "power of story," I'll throw myself under a bus.

Instead of talking about it, let's get out there – as Nike says: *Just do it*. Andy Crouch, editorial director of the *Christian Vision Project* at *Christianity Today* magazine, captured this concept well in a recent interview:

> Cultural transformation is something that a lot of Christians talk about and aspire to. We want to be part of transforming culture. The question is, how is culture transformed? Does it happen just because we think more about the culture, or because we pay more attention to culture? As I was thinking about cultural transformation I became convinced that culture changes when people actually make more and better culture. If we want to transform culture, what we actually have to do is to get into the midst of the human cultural project and create some new cultural goods that reshape the way people imagine and experience their world. So culture-making answers the

"how" question rather than just the "what" we are about question. We seek the transformation of every culture but how we do it is by actually making culture.

We ultimately *change* culture, by *making* culture. Defining it on our own terms and starting new conversations through media, entertainment, and art that expresses new vision and values.

Hopefully, this book will not only warn about the dangers of what we've been doing wrong in the media, but inspire many to re-consider how to do it right.

A good place to start is by looking at some of the most common criticisms of Christian media.

CHAPTER FOUR
THE CRITICISMS OF RELIGIOUS MEDIA:
WHAT THE AUDIENCE THINKS

> **TV EVANGELISTS SAY THEY DON'T FAVOR ANY PARTICULAR DENOMINATION, BUT I THINK WE'VE ALL SEEN THEIR EYES LIGHT UP AT TENS AND TWENTIES.**
> — DENNIS MILLER, COMEDIAN

Now that I've got all that stuff out of my system, let's get to why you bought this book.

My first encounter with David Kinnaman, president of the Barna Group, was in Vancouver, where we were keynote speakers for the national conference of a major Canadian evangelistic organization. The ministry was considering the possibility of moving their evangelism outreach into the media and wanted to hear our perspective. Since this was shortly after David's book *UnChristian* was published, they wanted him to address the perception of Christians in the culture, and present some background on how and why that perception came to be.

After David laid the groundwork on the cultural landscape, they wanted me to present media options – what was working, the future direction of media and what were the best alternatives in Canada for reaching large audiences with their message.

During the conference, my wife Kathleen and I became friends with David, and since that time, we've shared the stage at other events and crossed paths numerous times. If you haven't read *UnChristian*, I strongly recommend it. It's the sobering result of a Barna Group study that reveals how the secular culture views Christians today and the implications for evangelism.

When it comes to examining the Christian community, sources from David's book to national news magazines have lamented the downward spiral of the perception of Christians in the culture and indicating it's plunge to the lowest level in recent memory. There are plenty of reasons of course; it's not a simple issue.

Although Jim Bakker wasn't the first evangelist to fall from grace, because of his prominence in the media, his fall from ministry decades ago began a domino effect. Followed by evangelist Jimmy Swaggart, Pastor Ted Haggard, and many other smaller figures, these stories of sexual misconduct, financial misdeeds, and more have left a devastating wake.

In many ways, online search has created a revolution in accountability.

The search engine Google is less about "search" and more about "reputation management." In a digital, online world full of instant information, it's virtually impossible to hide anything. The drunk driving arrest in college, the bankruptcy, or your missed child support payments, will all be uncovered in a Google search. Many leaders from religion, business, and government have been brought down as a result of documents or photographs from the past that resurface in an online search.

Google is now a verb. "To Google" has become a permanent part of our lexicon.

I visited one pastor who pulled me aside and said, "It would be better if you didn't mention my yacht to any of my church members. I don't think they'd understand." I told him he was living in the Stone Age. I said it would only take a reasonably intelligent high school kid about 10 minutes to not only find out about the yacht, but by using Google Earth have a satellite photo of the boat sitting at the dock.

MEDIA IN A POST-ANALOG WORLD

Today we live in an age of instant access to information. With cell phones, text messaging, email, and technologies like Twitter, news travels fast. Even major news networks are in on the game. CNN created "News To Me" as an avenue for regular folks to send in "iReports" shot on their cell phones or home video cameras. I recently spoke at Erwin McManus' Awaken Conference in Pasadena, California. I learned later that as I was speaking on the stage, one of the audience members was using Twitter to send text messages of my comments to various contacts in his address book. Even as I was speaking, people thousands of miles away were writing blog posts about my talk in real time. *Before I walked off the stage, the blog posts were already online.*

The immediacy of technology has much to do with the brutal beating the perception of Christians has taken in our culture. We're simply flooded with information – good or bad – and with email, cell phones, text messaging, and other instant message capabilities, everyone sees everything.

And they see it right now.

In this era of instant information, where we're being bombarded with data, perception matters more than ever. In my book *Branding Faith* I present the case that in many ways, perception is the core of branding and identity. In a media-driven culture, it's not just who you are that counts, it's how you are perceived. Further, if you don't work to shape your perception, you'll spend the rest of your life at the mercy of other people who will.

Branding is powerful, as James B. Twitchell writes in his book *Shopping for God*:

> Once a brand choice is made, usually in late adolescence, it sticks for awhile. That's why most advertising (and the cul-

ture that it carries) is directed toward teenagers. It's been estimated that it costs about $200 of marketing to get a fifty-year-old to change his brand of beer, but only about $2 to get an eighteen-year-old to do the same. And the kid isn't even legal. In fact, if you look at beer advertising, you'll see that the target audience is well under the legal age, just as it is with cigarettes. Joe Camel was a kid's cartoon for a reason. Hooked early, the user will stay true – not to the product, but to the brand.

The truth is, a brand isn't what *we* say it is – it's what *they* say it is. In other words, it doesn't matter if you're a brilliant executive, or if everyone at your company believes you got the job because your father-in-law owns the place. It doesn't matter if you're a great writer or if everyone else thinks you're a no talent hack. Successful corporations understand the power of perception and how it can make or break a company.

THE POWER OF PERCEPTION

I've always been fascinated by Howard Schultz, the founder of Starbucks, not only for his vision, but for the way he designed the stores as a "third place" (after home and work). The design, attributes and products in every Starbucks store were carefully developed to this end; his desire to reflect a great coffee experience is notable. Recently, I was reminded that with thousands of workers, just how hard it must be for Starbucks (and other large companies) to train employees to live out the brand on a day to day basis.

At the Dallas-Fort Worth Airport, I ordered an iced soy latte from the Starbucks next to my gate. (My wife got me hooked on those things!) I first noticed something odd, when a sweet elderly lady in front of me asked for a drink that was clearly on the menu, but the cashier argued that the drink didn't exist. Trying to be nice, the lady kept pointing to the menu board, but the cashier wouldn't even turn around. He just kept saying there was no such drink. He grew more and more angry and impatient with the lady, who was becoming exasperated herself.

Finally, I leaned over and with a little more authority "asked" him to turn around and take a look, and sure enough, there was the drink, right on the menu. Rather than apologize to the customer, he just grunted and rung up the order without a word.

Next, as the barista was fixing my iced soy latte, she inexplicably started squirting caramel into the drink. I asked her what she was doing, and obviously annoyed, she replied, "Putting soy into it." When I told her that was caramel, not soy, she looked at the drink, put down the caramel bottle, picked up a spoon, and start trying to scoop the caramel out of the drink. She literally took the drink over to the trash, scooped about a third off the top, put the lid on it, and handed it to me. Pieces of caramel were still floating around, and my cup was only two-thirds full.

It was one of those truly amazing moments in bad customer service.

When I asked her to start all over, she just scowled at me, and refused to speak. She re-made the drink, but was clearly not happy about it. As I walked away, I noticed the same barista set up the next customer's drink without putting the top on correctly, so when the customer picked it up, it spilled everywhere. Once again, she just acted annoyed and didn't say a word.

At that moment, all the millions of dollars in advertising, creative marketing, store design, brilliant executives, and great products from Starbucks didn't matter to me. The entire brand came down to those two rude and indifferent employees. As I picked up my latte, the Starbucks brand wasn't what *they* say it is, it's *what I was experiencing at that moment.*

Remember the Jet Blue weather disaster of 2007 when so many of their jets sat on the runways for hours during the Christmas rush? During that customer service nightmare, none of Jet Blue's special ticket prices, advertising, innovative marketing, creative efforts, or anything else mattered. To those customers sitting frustrated on the planes, the flight attendants represented that brand, and in the airport, the ticket agents did the same. How those employees reacted to the crisis and the customers either built customer loyalty or destroyed it.

AUTHENTICITY, IDENTITY AND COMMUNITY

In the book *Buying In* author Robert Walker looks beyond the typical issues of *status* and *usefulness* to get to the root of why branding has such power over consumers. After all, can status really account for hundreds of millions in sales for a specific brand of cleaning products? Is an iPod really more useful than Microsoft's Zune?

Walker attributes branding's power to the triad of *authenticity, identity,* and *community.* He illustrates this point by looking at real-life case studies such as the re-branding and revival of Pabst Blue Ribbon beer in the 1990s, when it became associated with the blue-collar American heartland. In a similar fashion, skateboarding companies have made millions intentionally positioning themselves as "outsider" companies.

Awhile back, Kathleen and I attended a friend's wedding in Palm Springs, California the same weekend as a motorcycle rally, where 30,000 bikers ascended upon the desert city. While Kathleen was shopping downtown I started a conversation on the sidewalk with a biker who considered himself one of the last true "outlaws" on the road. As he told me how "independent and free" he was, and how he "answered to nobody," I was fascinated to see that every single article of clothing he wore sported the official Harley-Davidson brand. He had a Harley jacket, leather chaps, boots, helmet, and t-shirt – not to mention motorcycle. All Harley, all the time – *independent indeed*.

The Harley brand gave my biker friend a sense of community, and while his self-image as the *last great outlaw* was a bit exaggerated, it did give him a sense of identity. As a result, he will be a loyal Harley-Davidson fan for years to come.

PERCEPTION MATTERS

In his book, *A Purple State of Mind*, Craig Detweiler illustrates how perception changed a presidential election. In the first televised presidential debate on September 26, 1960, then Vice President Richard Nixon squared off against Senator John F. Kennedy. Detweiler describes the broadcast:

> Kennedy arrived at the debates looking tan, rested, and energetic. Nixon looked haggard, having recently fought off the flu. He refused to don makeup, figuring his forceful words would rule the day. Those who listened to the debate on the radio found Nixon the victor. Yet those watching the debate on tiny black and white televisions saw something else. They saw Nixon sweat while Kennedy smiled. Although Nixon was only five years older than Kennedy, his demeanor seemed comparatively ancient in outlook and energy. Nixon's noticeable five-o'clock shadow didn't help either.

As Detweiler reminds us, Nixon – coming from a print generation – realized the connection between style and substance far too late in the campaign.

In a media-driven world, how you're perceived is just as important as who you are.

How people perceive issues differently has always been a factor in human relationships. In his book, *Original Sin: A Cultural History*, Alan Jacobs notes the different reactions to evangelist George Whitefield's preaching throughout the English countryside in the 18th century. He points out that when Whitefield preached on original sin, an English aristocrat responded, "It is monstrous to be told you have a heart as sinful as the common wretches that crawl on the earth." By contrast, the description of soot-covered coal miners to the open-air preaching was: "The white gutters made by their tears... ran down their black cheeks."

Both heard the same message and witnessed the same event, but their perceptions were dramatically different.

Human relationships, products, and well-crafted brands are about perception, and when it comes to getting your message heard, a strong perception allows you to cut through the barrage of media clutter consumers must wade through on a daily basis.

Years ago, when Joel Osteen took over as pastor of his father's church, Houston's Lakewood Church, our challenge was to create a new program that would capture Joel's unique gifts and brand story. Working with Lakewood's music and television team, we created a theme based on the line, "*We Believe in New Beginnings.*" Using that as the starting point, we wrote a song, created a program opening, and developed the entire program and a marketing campaign around that concept. The perception in the community was indelible, and the Houston press would later call it one of the most successful marketing campaigns in the city's history.

THE POWER OF DENIAL

The problem is, too few national media ministries understand the power of perception. I once had a client that produced a weekly program that was broadcast on a national religious TV network. They were frustrated with many of the rules the network had in place – many of which admittedly seemed capricious at best. It was a common complaint I'd heard before from other programmers, so knowing the leadership team at the network, I set up a meeting for my client to meet with the network. As happens in so many cases, once you put people in the same room, and let them hear each other's perspectives first-hand, most disagreements can be worked out very quickly.

My client and I went to the network headquarters and met with various members of the programming team. We spent the day touring their facilities, learning why they make the decisions they do, and my client received an up close and very personal view of network operations. As a result – although a few differences remained – it completely changed his thinking. It helped him see the difficulty of managing a 24/7 broadcast schedule and managing so many national programs. As a result of the meeting, my client completely changed his attitude toward the network.

It was such a revelation, I immediately sent an email to my friends at the network thanking them and letting them know what a success it had been. In fact, I encouraged them to have a yearly "network open house" so all their programmers could come in, tour the facilities, learn their policies, and have a personal look at how and why they made their decisions. I even suggested to one of the younger leaders that he could use this new forum to share his vision for the future of the network.

One of the network executives I copied on the email liked the idea so much that he sent it on to the founder of the network.

Bad idea.

It wasn't long before I received a blistering two page letter from the founder, attacking me for the *audacity* to think there were actually people out there who didn't like their network! How dare I tell them people were unhappy with his network – it is for the Kingdom of God! *Everyone* loves his network! He also made it clear that he didn't give a rip about the young executive's vision for the future of the network. After all, the founder reminded me, he wasn't dead yet.

I kept the letter in my files because it's such an outstanding example of how a generation of Christian leaders simply don't understand perception.

He thinks the network is wonderful. He thinks it's doing a great thing. He thinks everyone loves it. But it's not about what *he* thinks – it's about what the *audience* thinks.

That particular network – along with many others that broadcast Christian programming – has the greatest of intentions. But intentions don't guarantee support, response or a following. Perhaps even more importantly – they don't guarantee a legacy.

Regardless of what we think of Christian media, there are millions who despise it, and for some good reasons. Maybe it's time we took a tour of some of the most common criticisms:

1) The Gold Furniture Syndrome: Cheesy, Corny and Tasteless
We don't have to run through the list of gold furniture, bad hairstyles, toupees, outrageous clothes, mountains of make-up – we've all seen it. Some of the founders of religious media were brought up in hard-core Pentecostal families where jewelry, make-up, and nice clothes were considered excessive, so when they became adults, they rebelled and went overboard.

Way overboard.

OK. Fine. But do we have to go so far? Tammy Faye Bakker may have won the gold medal in excess, but she's only the tip of the iceberg. There's no question in my mind that Tammy Faye did some wonderful things in her life, and I actually believe that she was (in a bizarre way) authentic. I do not doubt that her outrageous style attracted as many people to her as it turned away, and later in her life she was a powerful witness of unconditional love to the gay community.

However, to many her legacy – as far as her cultural perception is concerned – will always be her air-conditioned dog house, her outrageous lifestyle and of course, her make-up.

In chapter 5, I'll discuss my theory of the why Christian TV took on some of these over-the-top characteristics. If you work at a traditional media ministry – particularly one that's been successful over the last couple of decades – Chapter 5 will be particularly relevant to your situation.

I can't say enough about being real. As I wrote this book, broadcast journalist Tim Russert passed away unexpectedly from a heart attack. Among his many tributes, Russert may have been the last *normal* journalist left in Washington. In a tough town where reporters often assume a different persona, or allow their egos to take over, he stayed true to his values, his faith and his family.

As I look at the Christian media landscape, I often wonder how few *normal* people there are on Christian TV or on the radio.

> **WHAT MATTERS ISN'T THE POEM, BUT TO APPEAR ON TELEVISION AS A POET.**
> – GABRIEL ZAID, *THE SECRET OF FAME*

It's been said that Hollywood is brilliant at making fake things look real, and Christians are brilliant at making real things look fake. Authenticity matters. In a culture where design holds a powerful influence, taste – or lack of it – is noticed.

2) Giving to Get: The Prosperity Gospel

Many TV evangelists are rich because of greed, but not their greed. It's our greed. An earlier generation donated money to help those in need. Growing up, my mother taught us about those "less fortunate" and we gave because the Bible expressed great concern about the poor and suffering. But as I grew up, a concept came along that turned giving on its head. "Seed faith" teaching transformed everything we knew about raising money. The original concept was actually Biblical – based on planting a seed and expecting a harvest. But it completely changed our attitudes toward giving.

For the first time we weren't giving money to help others, we were giving to help ourselves.

The idea caught on, and with the instant global reach of Christian radio and television, it spread like wildfire. Not since the days in the early 16th century when the Catholic church sold indulgences (paying money for forgiveness of sins for you or your dead loved ones) has the cash rolled in and church leaders lived in such luxury.

Johann Tetzel, the most aggressive of the Dominican friars selling indulgences had a saying: *"As soon as a coin in the coffer rings, the rescued soul from purgatory springs."* It doesn't sound that different from today's, *"Plant a seed to meet your need."*

As the teaching grew, less trained pastors and leaders mixed in errors until some preachers created entire ministries around having a "financial anointing." (Try to find *that* in the Bible.) And they were in high demand for their ability to raise money on TV. If you watch Christian TV network telethons you'll often see the same financial "A-Team" marched out year after year. These are the guys that know how to make the phones ring off the hook, and believe me, they get results.

We let it happen because, by then, we had all become trained to believe that giving wasn't about helping *others*, it was about helping *ourselves*. So it didn't really matter if the preacher spent the money on luxury living. God was going to bless us, and that was all that mattered.

No matter what you believe about prosperity teaching, the real question is, after decades of this teaching, where does that leave us?

On the plus side, it's built some massive outreaches. There's little question that incredible influx of money created many of today's major ministries, Christian colleges, Bible schools, churches and radio and TV networks. And that's a good thing.

On the downside, we created a generation addicted to the rush. This audience (and I use that word on purpose) is now accustomed to feeding their addiction with gimmicks. They race to conferences looking for a "fresh anointing," as ministries desperately create more and more "Jesus junk" fundraising offers. The cycle never stops, because when you give to get, you have to get something even greater next time around.

For some people, I'm convinced it's not that different from an addiction to crack cocaine.

I've been in plenty of tense ministry meetings where the staff was frantic, trying to come up with a new "offer" (read gimmick) for their radio or TV audience. And they've come up with some pretty crazy ideas. I even have a shelf in my office with a collection of some of the more outrageous "Jesus junk" products I've come across.

However, I think something new is on the horizon. We're facing a generation that isn't so addicted. Younger people today have seen the excesses of giving to get, and they want nothing to do with it. They'd rather help a cause driven by U2's Bono than a TV evangelist.

THE GENERATION THAT WANTS TO MAKE A DIFFERENCE

Major churches and ministries are caught in the middle. Right now, their largest group of givers is still looking for gimmicks like prayer cloths, anointing oil, and little packets of seeds. But that group is dying, and a new generation is coming. Therefore, giving to get has not served Christianity well in the long-term. Although many TV evangelists live in personal luxury, many of their churches and ministries are now deeply in debt.

I won't candy coat it – the transition to the next generation of givers will be painful. Only if pastors and ministry leaders put their teaching in balance, and preach the real purpose for giving, do they stand a chance to survive.

Let's re-think giving to get, and start giving for the right reasons. Looking inward only feeds the addiction, but looking outward can actually change the world.

THE REAL MONEY PROBLEM

The truth is, the person who really transforms religious media won't be the creative genius, it will be the *funding* genius. The reason is a little understood concept called "paid time broadcasting."

In an earlier chapter I mentioned the journey Oral Roberts took when he went to NBC with his idea for "The Abundant Life Program" in 1954. At the time, as was standard practice, they brought in the usual suspects to advertise and sponsor the new program. In those days, advertisers had a great deal of influence over the programs they sponsored. Representatives from the sponsoring company could approve the script, crew, subject matter, and more.

I don't know what sponsors were brought in for "The Abundant Life Program," but whoever they were, the concept bothered Oral. If he was going to preach the gospel, he didn't want anyone from an outside corporation to tell him what he could and couldn't preach or how he could preach it.

So he cancelled the contract and went back to Tulsa.

But then he thought, "If a corporation can purchase that airtime, why can't I?" So he went back to NBC with the idea, and they said it had never been done before – but why not?

That's the day "Paid Time Broadcasting" was born.

It was a brilliant move, and allowed Christian television to grow to a national scale. Oral went out and raised the money – and then began offering books and other products on TV to pay for the time. It worked well because in those days there were only three TV channels, so there wasn't the massive competition for viewers that exists today. As a result, the response flowed in, and out of that flood, Oral Roberts University and many other global outreaches were born.

But then cable TV changed everything.

In the late 1960s, advertisers began to tell broadcasters and programmers, "I don't care what you put on the air, just deliver me an audience."

They were looking for eyeballs. Lots of them.

Advertisers moved away from *influencing* content, to simply *sponsoring* it. That was when Christian broadcasters should have gone back to Madison Avenue advertisers and said, "Bring on the sponsors, and we'll allow them to pay for our programs." But with limited radio outlets, and only three TV channels (which meant no competition), Christian broadcasters were making plenty of money just the way it was. Why rock the boat?

But something new was rumbling, something that would change the paradigm forever – cable television. The advent of cable television eventually splintered the three major broadcast networks into multiple channels. As I write this, our cable company in Los Angeles offers 500 channels, and even in the most remote places in America, people can access multiple channels through various cable or satellite providers.

With so many channels splitting up the audience, advertisers felt there wasn't a big enough audience anymore to justify their sponsorship of Christian media. So now in the 21st century, Christian television is still stuck in the "paid time" model that essentially hasn't changed since 1954 (incidentally, the year I was born).

The religious broadcasting model hasn't changed, but the media world has.

Oral Roberts, Billy Graham, Jimmy Swaggart, Rex Humbard, and Robert Schuller had little competition in those early days. Today the landscape has changed. Not only are there many more national ministry programs, but every town in America seems to have multiple local churches broadcasting as well. As a result, launching a traditional television ministry these days is extremely difficult, if not nearly impossible.

With that paid-time model in mind, today the most common methods for financing traditional religious programming are:

Transactional
This is about offering books, DVD's, or other teaching materials and/or resources throughout the program. I'm a big believer that people need to read more, listen to great teaching, and digest the scriptures. So I'm a great advocate of offering your products and resources on your website, radio, or television programs.

Selling products is also the best way for new or emerging media ministries to raise money. Since they don't have a mature mailing list for donor development, creating popular products is an excellent way to generate support.

However, while I'm all for getting your teaching materials into the hands of the people, it is this kind of pressure that keeps the flood of "Jesus junk" product offers on the air and makes some programmers do some pretty weird (creatively *and* theologically) things to get a response.

It is also worth nothing that transactional customers don't always make the best donors. Often listeners or viewers that purchase a product are only interested in that particular product, and not in supporting your ministry. From a long-term perspective, it's more difficult to convert transactional customers into regular donors.

Donor development

This is about asking for financial support to gather names so a back-end direct mail program can develop that donor relationship into long term donors. This is the goal of telethons, as well as personal "asks" or requests for financial gifts. As most major media ministries would confirm, religious media is driven by direct mail. Radio or television may serve as the "connection point" of initial contact, but it is a direct mail campaign that actually converts someone from an initial contact into a partner or supporter of the ministry.

Partnership

This is the holy grail of fundraising: when your audience believes in your vision for ministry to the point that they'll support you on a regular, monthly basis. When this happens, it's not about products or campaigns, it is about creating such a compelling vision for your ministry that you build a support base that sticks with you through thick and thin. This is the donor relationship that makes the most significant difference in successful media ministries today.

Obviously this is an over-simplified explanation of fundraising strategy, but it's a good overview of the three main areas of focus. There are some rare cases where innovative local religious broadcasters are partnering with local companies and organizations for commercial sponsorship, but in the vast majority of cases – until we can successfully change the funding model – we'll continue to see these techniques (transactional, donor development, partnership) for a long time to come.

The real challenge is moving your audience through what I would call the "Donor Development Funnel." The steps involved in that process are:

Viewer Awareness: How do I break through the "media clutter" and connect with the appropriate audience? How do we get our cause or organization on their radar?

Evaluation: Can I get the audience to consider the value of my church, ministry, or non-profit? How can I connect with them on the basis of shared ideals and values?

Urgency: How can I make my project or organization a priority for our audience? How can I move them from evaluation to action?

Transactional: Will they donate or buy a product at least once? How can I at least urge them to move to a trial basis? (Getting your product or information into their home is a key first step in developing a longer relationship.)

Partnership: Can we develop such a sense of trust that they join with us on a regular basis to accomplish our project or continue our work?

This last step is about true *relationship*. **And relationship is crucial** in moving your audience or congregation through these steps to develop a loyal base committed to accomplishing your vision.

THE GROWING DEBT BURDEN IN TRADITIONAL MEDIA MINISTRIES

At this point, we need to discuss the increasing debt that a number of today's major traditional media ministries maintain. When allegations of mismanagement were made against the president of a major Christian university recently, one of the revelations, according to local news sources, was the school's approximate debt of $55 million. Recently, another major religious organization was seriously in debt, and may have only been saved when the founder died and they were able to cash in his life insurance policy. Other ministries that are considered popular in religious media are shouldering mountainous loads of debt – the amounts of which would most likely shock and upset their audiences.

Is this a problem? And if so, what does it tell us?

Thoughout the course of my career, it's been very rare for donors and supporters to give to erase debt. In the vast majority of cases, donors want to support ongoing projects. They're interested in the future, not the past. They give to build, expand, or otherwise accomplish a mission, but few people will give to eliminate debt, and even when they do, they rarely do it more than once. My experience is that donors feel like, "You got yourself into it, so get yourself out of it." They also don't feel erasing debt accomplishes anything positive, so it's not uncommon for ministries who are in the red to raise money for other projects and use some of it to keep their debt at manageable levels.

This tells me that some leaders haven't been sensitive to changes in the culture. Right now, we're going through the greatest generational shift in a long time, and many ministries who were very successful a generation ago, are struggling today. For instance, in previous generations, all you had to do was build a building, and people would give. Not so today. In spite of that, some older leaders still build, even though the money has dried up.

They're pouring new wine into old wineskins. Old strategies don't work with new audiences and new donors. The truth is, change happens. And if churches, ministries, and non-profits aren't aware of those changes or cannot adapt, they will suffer.

It's interesting that a number of these "old school" ministries are the ones teaching prosperity. This isn't the place for a discussion about the positive or negative aspects of prosperity teaching, except for the fact that apparently with a number of prosperity ministries, it seems to work for the leader, but not for the organization.

So, what do we do about it, you ask?

Here are a few thoughts:

Have the courage to close the ministry doors.
Nowhere does it say that a successful ministry or organization has to continue forever. One leader was famous for saying, "Success without a successor is failure." Says who? Why can't God raise up a great work for a particular generation or task and stop it there? Have the courage to say we've done a great work, accomplished our assignment, and now it's time to move on. The typical problem with this thinking is that too many people are on the payroll, too many people are making a living off the donations of the partners. In those cases, the ministry has ceased to be *mission-driven* and become *payroll driven.*

I think an even greater tragedy is the pressure on a son or daughter to continue their famous parent's vision. Certainly some children have the gifts, talents, and calling to continue the organization for another generation, but I've also seen tragic cases where the son or daughter wasn't remotely gifted like their parent, but succumbed to the pressure to carry the mantle. In some cases, it ruins their lives, never allowing them to discover their real calling or purpose until it's too late.

Closing the doors takes courage, but it could ultimately result in a new ministry springing up, or shifting donor dollars to another organization that's making a positive difference in the world. The bottom line is simple: there is no shame in recognizing when a specific ministry or project is finished.

Don't be ashamed of scaling back.
Evolve. Needs change, and perhaps your organization needs to change to meet those needs. Adjust. Scale back. Downsize. There is nothing wrong with that. Branding teaches us that becoming more focused often generates greater results.

We live in the era of the niche. Massive ministries who once had a broad mandate for evangelism, missionary work, or education should consider narrowing that mandate into a more focused area in the future.

I often ask clients, "What could you potentially be the best in the world at doing?" Find your niche – from spiritual, skill, and geographic standpoints. What area of ministry can you focus on, what particular skill can you exploit, and what location can you explore that's underdeveloped?

Perhaps in the 80s you were one of the largest media ministries in the country, but today you should focus on something smaller – still significant – just smaller. In a media-driven culture, it's all about the niche.

Re-think your purpose.
Esso became Exxon. Cingular became AT&T. Bill Gates started out building computer hardware, and when that didn't work, he shifted to software and changed the industry. Each generation is gifted in different ways. Founders need to realize that, and value the gifts and talents of the next generation. Allow your strategies to shift as the landscape changes. Don't be locked into a 30-year-old vision.

Get new insight.
Leadership expert John Maxwell calls it "fresh eyes." Sometimes it's important to get outside opinions, advice and expertise. Get a consultant's opinion. We live in the age of outsourcing. Not every organization can do everything well, and it can be far more beneficial to bring in experts for help than to try and do it all. Remember, you might not be able to afford a highly trained

and expensive employee on a full-time basis, but you probably could pay less for an equivalent part-time consultant.

Find someone you admire and hear them out. Never get so big you stop listening to smart people.

When it comes to outsourcing, it's important to realize that all organizations – both for-profits and non-profits – have become much more complex. In a flat world of government regulation, digital media, and globalization it's difficult for a single organization to do everything well. For some, it's a matter of expertise – seeking the best and brightest minds to help your organization succeed. For others it's about off-loading – keeping your workforce small and nimble, without sacrificing growth and productivity.

As you think about what you can – and can't – outsource, here are a few issues to consider:

- **With consultants and freelancers, you get access to the best people in the industry.** These folks have vast experience and expertise. They live independently, so they must be pretty good. After all, if they weren't any good, people wouldn't be hiring them.
- **From an administrative perspective, it's nice and neat.** No overhead, no benefits, no moving expenses, no tax deductions, no HR problems or bookkeeping. Pay the invoice and it's done.
- **A network of relationships.** Consultants frequently have wider industry experience than in-house people, and can call on the knowledge and experience of a wide circle of business contacts.
- **In an age of PR nightmares, the smaller your full-time staff, the less the chance for sexual, financial or other problems.** God forbid, but if a freelancer gets arrested for soliciting sex from a prostitute, since he's not a full-time employee, you have more legal protection and less PR damage.

There are certainly duds in the world of consulting, and I always recommend doing your homework, but in a digital world, getting outside perspective and advice is mandatory.

3) Demographic Targeting: Put It In the Trough Where the Pigs Will Eat It

Early in my career, I was hired to write a TV commercial script to promote a prominent evangelist's new book. When I turned in the script, the client rejected it outright. When I asked why, he shamelessly replied, "Phil, you're a good writer, and this script is written way too well. You have to learn to dumb it down for our audience. In other words, you have to put it in the trough where the pigs will eat it."

I understood his point of writing with simple clarity, but his explanation told me a great deal about how he viewed the very people who were supporting his ministry. Since that time, I've always been sensitive to the attitudes ministry leaders have toward the audiences they're supposed to serve.

THE CONSUMER IS NOT AN IDIOT, SHE IS YOUR WIFE.
— DAVID OGILVY, ADVERTISING LEGEND

It doesn't take much channel surfing – especially in the morning – to see that outside of the normal full-time religious television channels, some TV evangelists seem to be ganged up in blocks. Upon closer examination it seems those "ministries" (which some would call "fringe") who spend the whole program talking about and asking for money seem to be all gathered around the early morning block on BET – the Black Entertainment Television Network. So here are the guys who are the most aggressive about asking for major financial donations (my favorite is the "$1,000 seed") who seem to be aimed directly at inner city viewers. Does that mean these hard core prosperity ministries are targeting lower income, elderly, or minority viewers?

Interesting question, right?

How do I know? Look at the audiences. When these programs take a wide shot of their services, take a look at who's in the crowd. The vast majority of the audience members appears to be minority grandmothers. These are people who don't need to be sending $1,000 to a TV evangelist.

Now I'm not talking about all media ministries that broadcast on BET. That particular network has been very welcoming for religious programmers, and some of my clients are there for good reasons. My beef is with the "$1,000 seed" guys hawking Jesus junk – the TV evangelists who claim they have a "financial anointing" and only talk about how you need to send them your money.

Here's the issue for me. Yes, we live in a free country, and programmers – no matter how offensive – are free to broadcast in whatever available timeslot is successful for them. (Outside family hour issues of course.) If low income seniors, or anyone else for that matter, want to send these guys money, that is their choice, no one's putting a gun to their head.

I'm for as little regulation as possible when it comes to media, but these are supposedly *Christian* ministries. We have a hard enough time in our culture trying to keep Christians from looking like con-artists and crooks. So could we just get a little help here?

The issue of money and ministry is coming to a head. If media ministries can't restrain themselves, the government is going to do it for them. And these "financial miracle" guys will have pulled the trigger on the starting gun.

> **UNLIKE SO MANY, WE DO NOT PEDDLE THE WORD OF GOD**
> **FOR PROFIT.**
> – PAUL OF TARSUS, 2 CORINTHIANS 2:17 (NIV)

4) Jesus Junk

If you've read *Branding Faith* or ever heard me speak, then you know how much I despise what I call "Jesus junk." I collect some of the more outrageous junk – perhaps when I retire, I'll start a museum.

To be honest, offering crazy trinkets on television in exchange for a financial gift may be the single most significant reason the culture looks at religious media with disdain. You know the stuff I'm talking about– vials of anointing oil and "miracle water" are still big, as well as prayer cloths and miracle seeds among others. One TV "prophet" will even give you a "personal prophecy" (once you call and give him your credit card number of course).

I always ask the question: How did it come to this? How has the historic Christian faith that defeated the Roman Empire, changed nations and transformed the Western world denigrated to cheap trinkets, cheesy gimmicks and religious trash? We can always criticize the TV evangelists who pitch this stuff (and we should), but the fact is, there's an even bigger culprit – us.

Pardon me while I continue to rant. Because the truth is, we've created a generation of Christians looking for a magic bullet. That is why people will travel thousands of miles from conference to conference just to "get a word," find "fresh oil," "get the glory," or "catch their blessing." The truth is, they're looking for the easy way out.

We've become addicted to the feeling, and if we're going to encounter this culture with any real power, we have to do better.

Do I believe in miracles? Absolutely. I also believe the book of Acts when it says handkerchiefs that touched Paul were taken to the sick and they were healed. But Paul didn't have them mass-marketed and used for a fundraising scheme. I even believe God prospers people. But I also believe the Christian faith should not be about chasing a blessing or getting a word. It's about taking up our cross. It's about, as the Apostle Paul said, *"Knowing Christ and the power of his resurrection and the fellowship of sharing in his sufferings, becoming like him in his death, and so, somehow, to attain to the resurrection from the dead."*

There. Thank you. I feel better now.

5) Sleeping Pill TV: Boring, Boring, Boring

Earlier, I discussed the history of Christian broadcasting and pointed out that preachers seized the moment in the earliest days of the media. However, as wonderful as their messages might be, putting preaching on television simply is not the most effective use of the medium.

THE MEDIUM IS THE MESSAGE

In *Branding Faith*, I wrote about Canadian media theorist Marshall McLuhan, whose remarkable theories and ideas about media were all the rage on college campuses in the 1960s and 1970s. As the director of the National Association of Educational Broadcasters' Media Project, he pointed out: "Television is teaching all the time. It does more educating than all the schools and all the institutions of higher learning."

It was his seminal book, *Understanding Media: The Extensions of Man*, that was regarded as the holy grail of culture studies. He coined the terms "global village" and "age of information," long before the Internet. His work has inspired some of the greatest media pioneers of our time.

The most powerful of McLuhan's pronouncements was this statement: "The medium is the message." In other words, the way (medium) we choose to deliver a message has a significant impact on the message *itself*. In the church, we often say that the message never changes, but the method or medium does. I've heard that phrase over and over again, as a call to action, emphasizing the importance of continually embracing technology and new media in an effort to keep the gospel message alive in the culture.

It sounds good, but if McLuhan is right, it's not true at all. Perhaps the most significant expression of this thinking is his statement, *"The content or message of any particular medium has about as much importance as the stenciling on the casing of an atomic bomb."* McLuhan believed that the medium used to deliver the message is actually *far more important* than the message itself.

That's pretty tough to swallow, but worth serious consideration.

"TECHNOLOGY CHANGES, BUT THE MESSAGE DOESN'T" – IS A MYTH

The idea that it's OK to use different media to spread the gospel message, as long as we keep the message the same is a long-standing myth that we (finally) need to put to rest. It is a concept born of good intentions – because an earlier generation of Christians feared that using new technology to share the message of the gospel would compromise the message, and water down theology. As a result, early pioneers decided that as long as the message stayed the same, then using new technology was a God-send that should be utilized whenever possible.

It may be a fine nuance, but it's worth understanding, because it's been a key reason so many have turned their backs on Christian media. According to McLuhan, the medium does indeed change the message – *perhaps not from a theological perspective, but it does change it in a very significant and profound way.*

Program writers, directors, and producers found this out during the early days, transitioning from radio to television. When television was first invented, most scripts were simply radio dramas with pictures. In other words, there wasn't much visual action – directors just shot actors standing around talking to each other. It was flat and lifeless, and the audience wasn't impressed.

That's when someone finally recognized that television was something altogether new. That realization paved the way for what we now call "The Golden Age of Television" – the period from 1949 to 1960 – which is still considered one of the greatest eras of television programming.

I can't emphasize enough how important this idea is to understanding the current climate of religious media. In the book, *Amusing Ourselves to Death*, media critic Neil Postman discusses the impact form has over content:

> To take a simple example of what this means, consider the primitive technology of smoke signals. While I do not know exactly what content was once carried in the smoke signals of American Indians, I can safely guess that it did not include philosophical argument. Puffs of smoke are insufficiently complex to express ideas on the nature of existence, and even if they were not, a Cherokee philosopher would run short of either wood or blankets long before he reached his second axiom. You cannot use smoke to do philosophy. Its form excludes the content.

WOULD JESUS HAVE LEFT THE DEAD SEA VIDEOTAPES?

In 1977, British journalist Malcolm Muggeridge echoed McLuhan and Postman when he wrote, *Christ and the Media*. His purpose was to examine whether or not Jesus – had he been born in the present day – would have left the "Dead Sea Videotapes" rather than the Dead Sea Scrolls. He was very careful to point out that directing, shooting, lighting, and editing techniques can be so manipulated, that television is inherently a lie:

> The most horrifying example I know of the camera's power and authority, which will surely be in the history books as an example of the degradation our servitude to it can involve, occurred in Nigeria at the time of the Biafran War. A prisoner was to be executed by a firing squad, and the cameras turned

up in force to photograph and film the scene. Just as the command to fire was about to the given, one of the cameramen shouted 'Cut!'; his battery had gone dead, and needed to be replaced. Until this was done, the execution stood suspended. Then, with his battery working again, he shouted 'Action!', and bang, bang, the prisoner fell to the ground, his death duly recorded, to be shown in millions of sitting rooms throughout the so-called civilized world. Some future historian may speculate as to where lay the greatest barbarism, on the part of the viewers, the executioners, or the camera. I think myself that he would plump for the cameras.

However, he admits that we shouldn't throw out technology altogether when he says,

Does this mean that the camera and all its works are wholly evil and incapable of fulfilling God's purposes? Of course not...It's very nearly impossible to tell the truth in television, but you can try very hard. As far as the word is concerned, spoken or written, it has been used, and continues to be used, for purposes of deception, and for evil purposes like pornography. This is absolutely true. But, you see, a word comes from a man. Putting it in its simplest terms, if I write a novel, signed by my name, I am saying these are my thoughts, these are my views, these are my impressions, and the response of the reader is according. If you set up a camera and take a film, that is not considered to be anybody's views, that is reality, and, of course, it is much more fantasy than the words. Supposing there had been a film made of the life of our Lord. Do you think that that would have stirred men as the Gospels have?

I respect Muggeridge's views because of his credentials as a journalist and Christian. He presents a balanced argument, but also gives us reasons for great caution. As a journalist of his era, he was a print man, no question, and found the transition to film and video challenging at best.

He once wrote about a story by Soviet labor camp survivor Alexander Solzhenitsyn, about a desperate man in the bunk above his who, *"...used to climb up into it in the evening, and take old, much-folded pieces of paper out of his pocket, and read them with evident satisfaction. It turned out that they had passages from the Gospels scribbled on them, which were his solace and joy in that terrible place. He would not, I feel sure, have been similarly comforted and edified by re-runs of old footage of religious TV programs."*

I used both of those quotes in my earlier book *Branding Faith* and I repeat them here because the issue is so important, and the application to Christian media could not be more clear. When you experience a live worship service, the encounter can be powerful. As you sit in a sanctuary filled with hundreds or thousands of people, you feel the energy of the crowd, see the preacher before you and hear the choir fully engaged. You can see the pastor sweat, feel the pulse of the throbbing music and experience the reaction of the audience.

It can be a powerful experience.

But when you watch that same service later on television, it's a completely different experience. Certainly the words of the message are the same, but the live encounter you had is completely different now as you watch the service through the TV screen while eating dinner, getting dressed, reading a magazine, or talking to a friend.

The same is true for radio – hearing a service broadcast on the radio while driving in your car, or listening to it broken up into multiple podcast episodes does not have the same impact as your original experience sitting in the sanctuary. It would be different still if the message were transcribed into a magazine article or book.

Some might say that it's still the same content – just different expressions of that content. But the truth is – the expression impacts the content. Do you have the same visceral and emotional reaction to watching a sermon on TV and experiencing a live worship service?

Absolutely not.

THE MEDIUM IMPACTS THE MESSAGE

As a result, Christian media is still dominated by preaching – even after all these years. In spite of the fact that a "talking head" experience – especially on television – can potentially be the most boring experience in the world, we continue to fill the airwaves with the types of programming people hate the most.

Believe me, although most network executives don't have religious backgrounds, in my experience most are not "anti-religious." They are business people and their work is focused on making a profit. Therefore, if talking head preachers generated huge audiences, then trust me, major network prime time would be filled with TV preaching.

But Christian media *is* dominated by preachers, and while I personally think there should always be a place in Christian media for great preaching, its dominance on television and radio will eventually be its demise.

And by the way – the doctrinal compromises that an earlier generation feared now occur all the time because we refuse to understand the unique demands of the medium. I've spoken before about the "A-Team" that is brought in to do the heavy financial lifting during telethons. The truth is – behind the scenes – most TV network and station owners don't really care much for most of these guys. I've been in plenty of meetings where they were criticized by station and network management for manipulating Scripture to get the phones to ring. But because the financial cost of television is so excessive, as soon as telethon time comes around, guess who gets invited back?

6) Your Grandfather's Program: It's Way Too Old Fashioned
From a young person's perspective, most religious media programs today are answering questions no one is asking. There's no doubt that Christian radio and television have come a long way, and having attended the National Religious Broadcasters Convention over the years, I've seen that change firsthand. In fact, at the 2008 NRB conference, I was powerfully confronted with the progress. As I walked through the exhibit floor, I came upon a long time stalwart of Pentecostal Christian broadcasting. He'd been on numerous radio and TV programs over the years, and even though he is now aging, I noticed he hadn't lost a bit of that classic TV preacher style.

He was wearing a suit that was bright, flaming yellow, with little curlicue designs on the lapels. He was also sporting a white necktie, white belt, and matching white shoes. His bouffant was on full display – twisting around the back to cover any bald spots, and finishing with a magnificent curl on the top.

As I stood there, I realized it was a defining moment. In past years, guys like me in jeans and T-shirts were rare at a gathering of religious broadcasters, but now, *this* guy stood out like a sore thumb. At that moment, I realized that we've been making serious progress.

But there's still so much more to be made.

How many Christian radio and TV programs today answer the real questions of this generation? How many are truly willing to tackle current issues like homosexuality, abortion, racism, or social justice by *engaging* rather than *attacking*? How many can look at politics from the perspective of both political parties? From the viewpoint of most religious media programming, to become a Christian, you'd have to join the Republican party and the National Rifle Association.

This generation doesn't understand why Christian media is so po-larized, closed-minded and one-sided. They want a discussion, not a lecture.

Unfortunately, we've discovered that we can raise more money by focusing on an enemy. I'm convinced you'll never win a gay man to Christ by calling him names on national TV, but it will sure get some audiences worked up enough to write a check.

WANT TO RAISE SOME MONEY QUICK? GET UPSET ABOUT SOMETHING

We have plenty of preachers attacking various social causes, sin, and lifestyles – and don't get me wrong – sin is sin. But are we attacking it to make a difference, or get a response? This is especially true when it comes to boycotts, and plenty of major denominations and media ministries have used the boycott tactic over the years. Christians are quick to boycott the enter-tainment industry, corporations that support gay rights, left-wing organizations or a wide range of liberal causes.

The problem is, I haven't seen a shred of evidence confirm-ing that boycotts bring people to a saving knowledge of Jesus Christ.

After all, if it worked so well, why aren't missionaries us-ing the technique? Why don't missionaries surround a tribe in a third world country and boycott it? And while they're at it, let's call the tribe names, and criticize their beliefs. Missionaries don't do it because it doesn't work. Simple as that.

Years ago, and with a great deal of fanfare and publicity, a religious denomination initiated a boycott against a major Hol-lywood entertainment company. The problem was during the boycott the offending company's sales went up. A few years later, a senior leader of the denomination called me for advice on how to delicately call off the boycott without making the denomination look foolish.

The respective leadership of both organizations met together, and after shaking hands, they both declared victory.

The truth is the boycott did absolutely nothing.

IT DOESN'T WORK FOR EVANGELISM, BUT IT DOES WORK FOR RAISING MONEY

Creating an enemy, then calling an all out war on that enemy really gets a segment of the Christian population worked up. The problem is the perception that is left in its wake. Today, Christians are known as the *people who are against everything*, when in truth, we're telling (as the movie title describes) the greatest story ever told. If anything, we should be known as the people who are *for* something – something positive that can transform lives and impact the culture.

Young people understand this very well. They've been raised on the media and they are the most pitched, advertised, and sold-to generation in history. They've been branded since birth, and they know a hard sell when they see it. This generation has seen the excess and rarely falls for it – a fact Christian media ministries are discovering right now.

When it comes to creating an "enemy," you must first ask yourself about your ultimate purpose. For instance, if you're trying to draw attention to a specific issue, such as homelessness, poverty, or moral decline, and mobilize the religious community to take action, then creating an enemy (that particular issue) might be the appropriate thing to do. For instance, when it comes to true evil, like human trafficking, it's perfectly appropriate to name the evil for what it is, and mobilize a group to make a difference.

My only caveat is that while it's OK to make an enemy of an issue, it's never appropriate to create an enemy out of a person or a community.

Too often Christian media leaders get it backwards and end up demonizing a particular group of people. In that case, it always comes back to haunt them later. Those with experience on the front lines of ministry and evangelism know that you'll never win a person to Christ through criticism or name-calling. The challenge is knowing your audience, and speaking appropriately to that particular audience.

> AM I ARGUING THAT PEOPLE OF FAITH SHOULD NOT MAKE THEIR VOICES HEARD IN THE ARENA OF PUBLIC DISCOURSE? ON THE CONTRARY: I BELIEVE THAT PUBLIC DISCOURSE WOULD BE IMPOVERISHED WITHOUT THOSE VOICES. BUT WE SHOULD NEVER DELUDE OURSELVES INTO THINKING THAT "DOING POLITICS," TO USE SIDER'S PHRASE, REPRESENTS THE HIGHEST OR BEST OR EVEN A PROXIMATE EXPRESSION OF OUR PROPHETIC MISSION. A PROPHET ALWAYS STANDS AT THE MARGINS, CALLING THE POWERFUL TO ACCOUNT. MISPLACED ALLEGIANCE TO POLITICAL POWER REPRESENTS A FORM OF IDOLATRY, AND THE FAILURE OF EVANGELICALS GENERALLY AND THE RELIGIOUS RIGHT IN PARTICULAR TO CALL POLITICIANS TO ACCOUNT, ESPECIALLY THOSE POLITICIANS THEY PROPELLED INTO OFFICE, IS THE STUFF OF, WELL, SCANDAL.
>
> – RANDALL BALMER, REVIEWING RONALD SIDER'S BOOK, *THE SCANDAL OF EVANGELICAL POLITICS*

AUTHENTICITY

It's ultimately about *authenticity*, which in my experience is the defining characteristic of this generation. I recognized it when my daughter Bailey was in elementary school. During my career I've been asked many times to judge film and video festivals and competitions. Once, I was given the children's programming category, so I thought I'd have Bailey sit in and screen some of the children's programming with me. I figured she'd

enjoy it, and at the very least, give me some indication of its effectiveness.

It didn't take long after hitting the "play" button for Bailey to run screaming from the room. When I asked her about
it – now remember this is an elementary school kid at the
time – her reply was, "Dad, it's so cheesy."

Even elementary aged kids recognize when something's not
authentic.

> THIS IS A GREAT WAY TO START YOUR DAY AND BRING YOU
> THE CONFIDENCE YOU NEED TO STAND BEFORE THOSE
> WHOM YOU NEED TO FACE. WALK IN THE CONFIDENCE
> THAT HAS BEEN GIVEN TO YOU BY GOD ALMIGHTY AS YOU
> BATHE WITH THIS SOAP, KNOW THAT YOU ARE BECOM-
> ING MORE AWARE AND SPIRITUALLY GUARDED, SO THAT
> YOU CAN MEET LIFE'S CHALLENGES. THIS IS A SOAP THAT
> HELPS BRING PROTECTION AND GIVE YOU A GREATER
> ABILITY TO FUNCTION WITH GREATER INTUITION AND IN-
> SIGHT. REMEMBER, ACCORDING TO YOUR FAITH, SO BE IT
> DONE UNTO YOU.
>
> – ONLINE ADVERTISEMENT FOR "PROPHETIC AWARENESS SOAP"

When it comes to Christian *television*, many of the problems we still see today stem from a time when – in many ways – the medium reached its high point. I've already mentioned the role Oral Roberts played in the development of religious radio and television by taking his program to a major, national audience. In the early 1970s, that audience reached its zenith.

Between 1973 and 1975, I was a student worker for the Oral Roberts television ministry. I needed a job and I was a TV and film major, so it made sense. At that time, the ministry had just finished building the multi-million dollar Mabee special events center on the Oral Roberts University campus in Tulsa. It was designed as a combination basketball arena and state-of-the-art television production studio. Even as a novice in the industry, I was impressed by the vision and quality of everything the ministry created. They had purchased the first new batch of RCA studio cameras, which at the time were the absolute top of the line. From the cameras to lighting equipment, to post-production and more, we had just about anything a creative team could want or need to produce great television.

If that weren't enough, Ron Smith, the ministry chief of staff at the time, negotiated deals with major Hollywood behind-the-scenes talent, and flew in program directors, lighting directors, art directors, and other craftsman who were the best in the business.

It was a dream for a student like me to be working on a program where the department heads were Hollywood professionals. I started out as a grip (the crew that builds and moves around sets and equipment), then graduated to the lighting crew, and eventually became assistant director and cameraman. A few years after graduation – and a short stint working in Hollywood – I moved back to Tulsa and became the director of the program. It was a heady time for religious media.

During those days we were creating network quality prime time programs with popular special guests of the time like Dionne Warwick, Robert Goulet, Jerry Lewis, and Johnny Cash. During those years, Oral was easily the most popular national religious broadcaster on television.

With a weekly program broadcast on Sunday, and quarterly prime time specials, he never asked for money. He focused on family entertainment with an inspiring message, and with only three major networks, he reached a staggeringly large audience. Peggy George, the program's media buyer during that time, recalled that ratings varied according to the season and the particular program, but averaged 25 to 40 million viewers. George remembers, "This was a time before significant cable penetration and with very few religious stations, which we rarely used because of their low audience figures. I remember that our Sunday morning programs reached 4 million at the peak, running mostly at 9 or 9:30 a.m., and we were consistently the top-rated religious program at the time."

I'm often reminded of the sheer size of the general television audience during the three channel era. A number of years ago when so much was made of the large audience that viewed the final episode of "Seinfeld," I laughed. The final Seinfeld audience was smaller than the weekly audience for a *typical* episode of "The Beverly Hillbillies" back in the 1960s.

THE STYLE OF THE ERA

In the 1970s, when Oral's program was reaching 4 million people a week, it's important to note that it was also the peak of what we called "Variety" programming. The variety format was an entertaining mix of music, comedy, sketches, interviews, concerts – just about anything that worked. Everyone at the time was doing variety "specials" including performers like Johnny Cash, The Osmond Family, Carol Burnett, The Smothers Brothers, Don Rickles, and many more. Later, performers like Barbara Mandrell, Tony Orlando and Dionne Warwick picked up the baton before the variety run eventually came to an end.

One of the hallmarks of the variety format was *over the top performances*. After all, variety television had evolved from vaudeville, and many of the stars of variety programming hailed from comedy or vaudeville backgrounds. That intersection, coming on the heels of popular radio, combined comedy club talent, Broadway performers, recording artists and night club singers among others. It was a remarkable – if not larger than life – time in the history of television.

Two important things happened during this time that would forever change (for worse in my opinion) religious television:

First – the popular, over the top style was adopted by many religious broadcasters.
Exaggeration was the style of the day, and from music to comedy – even to simple interviews – it was all about *over acting and slapstick* in an effort to capture the audience's attention. Even

outside the variety genre, the most popular weekly programs were silly comedies like *Get Smart, Hogan's Heroes, The Beverly Hillbillies,* and *The Andy Griffith Show.*

That's why it's not surprising – particularly with Christian media personalities that came into their own during the 1970s and 1980s – that they've so often been criticized for being over the top, fake and inauthentic.

The religious producers weren't guilty of being *silly*, but they did dabble in *exaggeration*. They watched the over the top performances they saw on secular programming and translated that into exaggeration.

For instance:

> *When it came to music, it was all about grand spectacle.*
> *When it came to set design, it was all about ostentation.*
> *When it came to wardrobe, it was all about flamboyance.*
> *When it came to singing, it was all about over acting and emoting.*
> *When it came to budgets, who cares? There was plenty of money.*

Life was good in the world of Christian broadcasting. Audiences loved what they saw, donations flowed in and everyone was happy.

The Rex Humbard family was doing TV specials from Cypress Gardens, Florida; Robert Schuller was building the Crystal Cathedral; Oral and Richard Roberts did specials from Alaska to Hollywood; Jim and Tammy Bakker were just beginning to produce, perhaps the most over the top show of all, the Praise the Lord Club. (The *Charlotte Observer* dubbed it the "Pass The Loot Club.")

Then something terrible happened. The variety format started dying.

In the 80s and 90s, television changed, but guess what? Most Christian television personalities didn't.

The exaggerated, over the top style on television was eventually killed by dramatic changes in television, including 24 hour cable news and reality programming. With the advent of more and more non-fiction and reality shows hitting the airwaves, the audience came to enjoy seeing performers be *real*. They wanted them to be authentic and genuine – flaws and all.

When "Hill Street Blues" premiered in 1981, creator Steven Bochco took television in a new direction and there was no going back. Plots were messy. Stories were complicated. Issues didn't resolve neatly. The camera was always moving. It was a program about imperfect cops living in an imperfect world.

It was a show that changed television.

Television was changing. The problem was, it took a long time for Christians in the media to see the change, and to be honest, some still haven't noticed it.

Second – production design was a problem.

Television in the 1970s was part of the cultural transformation that grew out of the radical change of the 1960s, resulting in some truly awful fashion and design styles. When I enrolled as a freshman in college in 1972, my wardrobe was filled with outrageous plaid pants – remember the ones with the big cuffs? I had my fair share of platform shoes. I even had a friend with platforms so big he had a small fish aquarium in the clear plastic heel of his shoe.

It was the age of big hair and loud clothes. Fashion restraint was tossed out the door like yesterday's garbage. If you graduated in the 1970s, go pull out your high school or college photos and show your children – just be ready for ridicule and no small amount of humiliation.

To make matters worse, when Kathleen and I were married in 1977, I wore a *brown tuxedo*. Who wears a brown tuxedo? Only someone tainted by the toxic fashions of the time.

Christian television (and most religious personalities) adopted these same styles, so it's no surprise that big hair, outrageous clothes and strange furniture became the norm on Christian channels during this period. But fashion and styles changed, and once again, Christian's didn't. Even today, there's plenty of big hair, gold furniture, loud styles, and downright excess available 24 hours a day on many religious programs.

The negative baggage began because of its intersection with the most successful times in Christian television's history.

Long after the secular television networks had moved beyond the variety format, long after the production styles and fashions changed, I watched many media ministries dig in their heels. On more than one occasion I saw ministries teeter on the brink of bankruptcy because of their refusal to see the changes taking place. In some cases, the producers – *who had been so successful producing the major ministry programs of the 1970s* – struggled the rest of their careers because they never fully recognized the changing media trends.

The sad truth is – particularly with older media ministries – much of the thinking from this period still exists today, and that's why so much criticism is directed toward these programs.

It is not the message that is under attack, in most cases, it's the messenger.

You really have to understand just how huge the 1970s were for religious broadcasting to realize why they were so hesitant to let go. Oral Roberts, Rex Humbard, Fulton Sheen, and Billy Graham had been reaching massive audiences for years. Then Pat Robertson, Paul Crouch and Jim Bakker came on the scene with The 700 Club, Trinity Broadcasting, and Praise the Lord. More nationally known preachers like Robert Schuller and Jimmy Swaggart followed. The audience numbers and response were incredible, and the equipment, facilities, and productions were all highly professional. Even now, in meetings with old timers, they continue to look back on those days as the glory days of religious broadcasting.

As television and audience preference began to change, they refused to let go of the techniques and styles that were so successful in the 1970s. As a result, their once huge audience and strong response began to dwindle away. In spite of the shift, they *still* continued to resist change.

So having given you a little background, here are the warning signs – *the offenders* – that indicate your media outreach or ministry has fallen behind. This is especially important for traditional media ministries that may have been successful in the past. If you really want to reach a bigger audience (and the next generation) this is the list to avoid:

OFFENDER #1: You talk in a different voice when the camera or microphone is turned on.
Pastor Greg Laurie calls it "pulpit personality." Love it or hate it, reality programming has left an indelible mark on the industry. People now see what happens behind the scenes on HBO, they see "America's Favorite Home Videos," they see non-professionals on YouTube, and they watch the news 24/7 on cable. So when you appear on your program with your "classic TV voice" it sticks out – and not in a good way.

You know who I'm talking about. Numerous ministry leaders who are gracious, authentic and engaging when talking with friends over lunch, become someone else once the cameras are rolling.

The television commercial business is a great example of how television has changed. National spots used to be narrated by men with powerful, deep voices that resonated with power and authority. But listen to today's commercials; more often than not, they sound like regular guys or gals. Advertisers recognize that connection doesn't come from a perfect voice, but from the sound of someone the audience can relate to, someone like you and me.

Sometimes you'll hear the voice of a celebrity, but in most cases, they're hired not because of the quality of their voice, but because their voice is recognizable.

Watch regular television and listen to the difference. Stop trying to be bigger than life. Be real. Speak normally. It doesn't make you more anointed or powerful when you try to sound like God. Talk like everyone else, and you'll be amazed at the connection.

The "over the top" era is done.

OFFENDER #2: You wear a different hairstyle or clothes than everyone else.
Back in the glory days of "variety" programming, stars wore some pretty weird outfits, and the audience loved it. When I toured Graceland – the estate of the late Elvis Presley – I marveled at the collection of his outrageous concert outfits. Unbelievable stuff.

A walk through the historical section of a prop and costume department in Hollywood is a similar experience.

But that was a different time.

While I'm always open to change, as of this writing:
> Nehru jackets are done.
> Big gold chains are for hip-hop artists and gangsters.
> Everyone knows you are wearing a toupee. Trust me.
> T.D. Jakes is cool. White preachers that try to dress like him are not.
> T-shirts under sport coats went out with Miami Vice.
> Spandex is not for TV – ever.

And when it comes to TV evangelists, what's with the hair? Do I really have to elaborate? Years ago, I filmed one offender deep in the desert of the Middle East for a TV segment. The wind was raging, and his comb-over was so huge, he went through nearly a case of hairspray to keep it under control. When he was finished, his hair looked more like a NASCAR helmet. The desert sands were blowing all around him, and my crew was fighting to hold down the equipment, but that comb-over stayed firm without a hair out of place. If a nuclear attack had happened at that moment, I wanted under that helmet of hair.

Study the wardrobe and hairstyles of secular TV hosts today. It's remarkably normal stuff. Tasteful and subtle.

Now – quick – switch back to a Christian TV program. Ouch.

Now to be fair, let me turn the tables and say something to today's "hip" young pastors: *It's time to stop wearing those striped shirts with the shirttails out when you preach.* Wearing jeans and open collar shirts is fine, but styles change and it's time to change with it. Hundreds of young contemporary pastors today all look the same – jeans, striped shirts, tails out.

Oh and while you're tossing out those shirts, dump anything with big designs on it. You know what I'm talking about – the t-shirts with the big printed crosses, or the torn up sport coats with stuff written on them.

The point is – people change, trends change, and fashion changes. When every pastor in America looks alike, nothing is distinctive anymore.

OFFENDER #3: You use the phrases, "Shake the Nations," "Transform Your Life," or "Touch the World" more than once in a 30 minute TV or radio program.
Yes – I'll admit I was guilty of these offenses in my day, but I went into treatment and I'm better now.

The point is about hype. There's just too much of it in religious media.

When *every* CD set, book, or sermon from every preacher will change your life, then nothing will. The audience gets numb when the superlatives come in a continual flood.

I always coach actors that during a dramatic scene, speaking in a loud voice all the time actually lessens the impact of the scene. When someone talks loud continually, after awhile, the audience simply filters it out.

Talking loud has impact, only after you've been speaking in a softer voice.

Contrast matters – stop the hype

Yes, God can do amazing things. He can transform people's lives. He can shake nations. But be realistic about your products and your ministry. Let other people say nice things about you. Modesty is a virtue. You'll be amazed at the credibility you'll gain with the audience.

OFFENDER #4: The audience notices the furniture more than the speaker.

I was once asked for my thoughts on a particular Sunday morning program, and when I viewed the DVD, the first thing I thought was, "The set design must have cost an absolute fortune." Not because it was creatively designed, but because it looked so expensive.

It was almost all white, very elaborate, had a few gold touches, and generally, looked like the inside of a palace. For some reason I can't figure out, we've come to think that we'll gain more respect as Christian broadcasters if we create the illusion of a really expensive set.

I made two comments to the pastor. First – why should I financially support your media ministry? Your set makes it appear you have all the money you'll ever need. Second – this environment is so far removed from my daily life, I can't really relate to you or your message.

He didn't take my advice, and his viewership continues to drop. (Well – what did he expect?)

I love a great setting for a program and our company has designed and built some amazing sets for our media clients. When it's appropriate, set design can make a huge impact because it places your message in a complimentary setting.

Sets are important, but the program is about your message – not about you or your set. Keep that in perspective.

OFFENDER #5: Your talk show format includes a monologue, a live band and interviews.

The comedy greats like Carson, Leno, Letterman mastered the late night talk show format and the next generation is following in their footsteps.

So let's look at another approach. For some mysterious reason, certain Christian broadcasters think this format is sacred, and have tried it over and over and still haven't succeeded. But by contrast, Oprah, Dr. Phil, Glenn Beck and plenty others have produced successful interview programs without the need of a live band, monologue, or the other trappings of late night TV.

Be bold. Be innovative. Stop copying other people and explore the right format to showcase your gifts and talents – not look like someone else.

OFFENDER #6: You're still building altars of prayer requests viewers sent in.

It's done for one reason – to impress the audience with numbers. If the audience can see that thousands of people responded, and the evangelist has built an altar from the requests, then maybe I should send in mine as well (and include a check) or so the thinking goes.

As with most of these points, I'm sure this gimmick was thought up by well meaning people with the best of intentions. Truth be told, it was probably a good idea ONCE. A long, long time ago. But when the same thing is done over and over again, it simply loses its meaning.

An older generation was touched by big, expansive gestures, but a younger generation sees it for what it is – excessive manipulation.

Anytime you use an idea like this, make sure you're sensitive to the issues of manipulation and exploitation. As I'll say over and over throughout this book, we're creating media for a generation that's been sold to, marketed, and branded all their lives, and they're the most media savvy generation in history.

Be very careful; even a well-intentioned idea can be perceived as a gimmick or publicity stunt.

OFFENDER #7: The singing group on your program is called "The (insert name here) Singers."
I think this idea went out about the time of *Lawrence Welk* or *The New Christy Minstrels*.

In junior high I was in "The New Creation Singers" (not to be confused with the Gene Dalton Family Singers). In seventh grade it was cool. It's not now. The (insert TV evangelist name) Singers. You get it. Enough said.

The list of religious media indiscretions could continue (and maybe we'll follow up on my blog at philcooke.com), but you get my point. The production styles, creative ideas, fashion, and techniques that worked yesterday don't always work today.

Please remember that in listing these particular offences, I'm not commenting on the intentions or integrity of particular ministries who are still trying these worn out methods.   I have the greatest respect for anyone trying to share their faith with the culture. However, I'm commenting on the need to stop kicking a dead horse, and start looking at a new method of transportation. Our job as communicators is to see shifts in the culture and change and adapt accordingly so our message is as relevant now as it was yesterday – and will still be tomorrow.

CHAPTER SIX
WHAT'S DRIVING THE CHANGE:
THE "MILLENNIALS" AND BEYOND

> THE WORKPLACE HAS BECOME A PSYCHOLOGICAL BAT-
> TLEFIELD AND THE MILLENNIALS HAVE THE UPPER HAND,
> BECAUSE THEY ARE TECH SAVVY, WITH EVERY GADGET
> IMAGINABLE ALMOST BECOMING AN EXTENSION OF THEIR
> BODIES. THEY MULTITASK, TALK, WALK, LISTEN AND TYPE,
> AND TEXT. AND THEIR PRIORITIES ARE SIMPLE: THEY
> COME FIRST.
> – CBS 60'S MINUTES REPORT, "THE MILLENNIALS ARE COMING"

There is a major force in America that has much to do with the purpose of this book. It's a generation that's driving the change – not only in Christian media – but in *all* media, and every aspect of life. They're called the "millennial generation" and it's not an exaggeration to say they are changing everything we know about culture and the way people communicate.

The millennials are about 80 million strong, born between 1980 and 1995 and are rapidly taking over the culture from my own generation, the baby boomers. There are far more insightful demographic and cultural studies on the millennial generation than this one, but for the purposes of this book, we need to examine the millennials, since they will be the next generation of religious media consumers. I'm also fascinated with millennials because Kathleen and I have two daughters in this age group.

One of the defining characteristics of my baby boomer generation was an often distant relationship with our parents. After all, we were the Woodstock generation and pretty much rebelled against *everything*.

In my case, my father was a pastor, and although he was a excellent provider, we didn't really have much of a personal relationship growing up. My parents understood little about the changes happening in the culture, and made no real attempt to reach out and engage. The only summer my father found the time to take me to Little League tryouts, we showed up too late to register. Years later, when I competed in the North Carolina State High School Track and Field Championship, my father didn't even come to see me race.

I love my father, and he was a great pastor to our congregation, but even today, we have remarkably little to talk about. While it varies, I bet many other baby boomers have similar stories.

As a result, most of us decided to do the opposite with our children, so we tended to "hover" over our kids. The term "helicopter parents" was coined from the way overly concerned parents stay involved as their kids grow up.

In many ways, the defining statement about millennials is that when it came to sports, they were the generation that received trophies just for showing up.

These "trophy kids" are the most catered-to and doted-on generation in history. As a result, this is a generation that only takes "yes" for an answer. Do they need a job? Absolutely not – *unless it's on their terms*. In many cases, they'll show up for work at noon, because their personal time comes first. They've never actually punched a time clock, have no idea why they need to show up at the office at 9 a.m. and expect that they'll always come out on top – with or without extra effort.

That's not to say there aren't wonderful things about this generation. Millenials have high expectations about life; they possess extraordinary skill and natural aptitude with computers and digital media tools and they can multi-task at incredible rates.

It is not about right and wrong, but rather new and different. The fact is there is a major paradigm shift occurring as the baby boomers age and the millenials grow up. The future success of Christian media depends upon our ability to navigate this shift.

For me and my friends, moving back in with our parents after college would have been a major embarrassment. In fact, if that had been my only option, I would have preferred to live on the street. But for young people today, moving back home seems like a smart career move because it saves money.

Our generation was taught to fight our own battles – in fact, every year in elementary school I remember my father telling my teacher to feel free to discipline me any way he or she saw fit – physical or otherwise – and then let him know about it so he could follow up at home. If I got threatened by a bully, my dad told me that it was my problem and I needed to deal with it.

As millennials move into the workforce, it is becoming clear they did not grow up fighting their own battles. Employers are finding that when this generation is disciplined at work, they will often get a call from the employee's *parent*, scolding him for mistreating their (adult) child. As a *60 Minutes* report, quoted at the top of this chapter, reveals, "Mom isn't just your landlord – she's your agent." That means parents are negotiating deals and managing the careers of their millennial children – even as they become adults.

A fascinating sociological aspect of this phenomenon is that for thousands of years, adulthood traditionally began around age twelve. When women began menstruation or young men reached puberty, they were considered adults and were treated as adults by the surrounding community. It wasn't until 1956 that the term "teenage" appeared. Thanks to the evolution of pop music, "teenage" defined a growing youth culture that had been developing since World War II.

From that point, "adulthood" seemed to start at 16-years-old and later to 18-years-old. With the millennial generation, adulthood seems to be pushed back even further. After moving back in with the parents after college, at what point does adulthood begin?

One of the most important results of these changes is delayed adolescence. What will the impact on the economy, the workforce, and culture in general be when adulthood begins at 30?

This shift has impacted media as well. The boomer generation grew up with only three TV channels and a handful of radio channels. Whatever networks shoved down the tube, we dutifully watched or listen to – no questions asked. We didn't exactly have much of a choice. Today media choices are everywhere; not only is this generation more picky, but they want to interact with the media they choose.

Why listen to radio programming when you can program your own iPod with exactly what *you* like?

Why be concerned with TV schedules when you can TIVO your favorite shows and watch them *whenever you want*?

Why buy entire CD's when you can download individual songs? (Remember how we used to purchase an entire album just to hear one or two great songs? Millennials have no idea what that's like.)

Why own a TV at all when you can watch everything on your computer or digital media device?

At the famous Cannes Advertising Festival in France in 2007, the hottest topic was programming content for mobile phones. Right now, that's the most aggressively pursued media platform because of the sheer number of mobile devices throughout the world.

Popular TV programs like "Lost" have active websites and social networking communities that allow viewers to comment on the program – even to the point of influencing storylines. Producers today go so far as to shoot alternate endings, allowing viewer feedback to determine the finale of choice. After all, growing up voting for the next "American Idol" by texting on their cell phone, has shown this generation that their voice can be heard, and that it counts.

Then again, none of this is really new – except to religious media programmers.

Religious media desperately needs to respond to this shifting paradigm and so far, it's not going well. A previous generation was happy to listen to the latest sermons and pronouncements from Billy Graham, Robert Schuller, Jerry Falwell and Pat Robertson, but the millenials want to be part of a dialogue, they need to talk back or they won't be interested.

Today, it's not about how we communicate with the audience, it's about how they communicate with us.

For instance, when it comes to fundraising, some prefer the phone, others regular mail, and still others the web. The web offers more interactivity, so we're seeing a dramatic shift in that direction – particularly as we've seen with the comprehensive Internet fundraising strategies of recent political candidates. The future of fundraising is about finding the channel your potential audience wants to communicate through, and talking to them through that particular avenue. Otherwise, you'll lose them.

> **TECHNOLOGY ALLOWS MARKETERS TO GIVE CONSUMERS A VOICE. AND THAT'S A DRAMATIC AND POWERFUL CHANGE, AS LONG AS WE PAY ATTENTION TO WHAT OUR CUSTOMERS ARE SAYING. IN THE [TWENTIETH CENTURY], WE DID MONOLOGUE MARKETING. WE DID MOST – IF NOT ALL – OF THE TALKING. AND WE EXPECTED THE CONSUMER TO LISTEN. NOW, IN THE TWENTY-FIRST CENTURY, WE'VE MOVED TO A DIALOGUE. CONSUMERS WANT TO BE HEARD. IN FACT, THEY WILL NOT TOLERATE NOT BEING HEARD.**
>
> – JOHN HAYES, CHIEF MARKETING OFFICER, AMERICAN EXPRESS

Think of it this way: At a party there's a guy who's determined to be heard, so he starts yelling at people. Everyone else is having a conversation but he's standing there yelling. Who are you more interested in meeting? The screamer or the others having normal conversations?

Millenials are far more interested in the individual conversations than the loud voices.

9/11 AND THE INFLEXIBILITY OF RELIGIOUS MEDIA

Most religious media today is not only ignoring their audience, but also hopelessly unresponsive – even during a crisis. The morning of 9/11, I sent out a series of emails and faxes, nearly begging religious TV and radio stations nationwide to break away from their regular programming and respond to the terrorist attack at the World Trade Center in New York City. Traditionally, the programming schedules of most religious media outlets are so locked in they have little or no ability – or interest – in responding to immediate events. But 9/11 was so important, I felt if ever there were a time...

After watching the horrifying crisis unfold on television, I ran to my computer and sent out a memo encouraging local Christian TV and radio stations to do a number of things, including up to the minute reports on what was happening, invite local pastors and ministry leaders to talk about the spiritual implications and invite experts in Islam to discuss the unfolding story from that perspective, all in an attempt to explain what was happening.

The result was remarkable. Within minutes I started getting calls that stations were pulling their regularly scheduled programming and going "live" in response to the crisis. I reminded them that with their massive news operations, secular networks were more equipped to report the *facts*, so I suggested that religious media outlets report from a *spiritual* perspective – offering prayer, a biblical view, the prophetic implications, spiritual insight, and giving their viewers hope.

One station in Texas told me later they hooked up live via cell phone with someone who had actually been inside one of the towers when one of the planes hit. Others brought in local experts on the Middle East to discuss the implications of the tragedy, while others offered 24 hour prayer and counseling for viewers and listeners.

One Christian television network called to say they were going into an emergency production meeting and using my memo as an agenda to re-think their programming for the next month. Others created websites so audience members could respond and connect. Needless to say, the impact was immediate and nationwide. It gave me hope that Christian media could indeed break out of the old paradigm.

But since that time, with most stations, the spontaneity and creativity in programming has not continued. Within weeks after 9/11, most religious radio and TV stations fell back into their static schedules – and in spite of major elections, dramatic social issues and other historic events, they refuse to give the audience any real sense of immediacy or interactivity.

Whatever age they may be, most religious media outlets are still owned or managed by men and women with the baby boomer mindset. For them, media is a one-way conversation, because that's all they've known. But sooner rather than later, that paradigm needs to change, because the audience is changing – and the audience isn't happy with that they're seeing and hearing.

On my blog at philcooke.com, I recently conducted a survey about Christian television viewing habits. The blog is focused on the topics of faith, media, and culture and the vast majority of readers are involved professionals or at least profoundly interested in the intersection of faith and media. In spite of that orientation, the result of this particular poll was sobering:

I watch Christian television:
20 hours a week or more – 3%
10 hours a week or more – 4%
5 hours a week or more – 10%
1 hour a week or more – 18%
I don't watch Christian television – 49%
We should abolish Christian television – 18%

If 67 percent of people who read an online blog dedicated to issues of faith and media either don't watch Christian TV at all or would prefer it be abolished – can you imagine how the general public feels about it?

Earlier, I mentioned my friend David Kinnaman's remarkable book called, *UnChristian: What a New Generation Really Thinks About Christianity... and why it matters.* As president of a research organization, The Barna Group, David has a unique perspective. The book is the result of a three year research project into the perception of Christianity among the wider culture, and it opens with the sentence that defines the book: *"Christianity has an image problem."*

David and I have spoken together at several major events, and I've found him to be genuinely concerned about how the non-believing public views Christians and how that presents significant obstacles to sharing the gospel. At one event in particular, I had the opportunity to interview David on the role of religious media, how it's contributed to this mess, and if it can play a role in getting us out.

There's no question in my mind that the main findings of his book were birthed from the excesses of religious media over the last few decades. In his research, David found that the general public uses the following words to describe Christians:

Anti-homosexual – 91%
Judgmental – 87%
Hypocritical – saying one thing, doing another – 85%
Old-fashioned – 78%

Too involved in politics – 75%
Out of touch with reality – 72%
Insensitive to others – 70%
Boring – 68%

There are a number of Christian radio and TV programs today that would clearly exemplify each of these descriptors – and some that might represent them all. For the most part, traditional Christian media doesn't unify, it divides. It's about being *against* issues, not being *for* issues. It's about aligning the Christian faith with a political party or being *critical* of the culture rather than reaching out and *engaging* the culture.

> **MILLIONS OF YOUNG OUTSIDERS ARE MENTALLY AND EMOTIONALLY DISENGAGING FROM CHRISTIANITY.**
> – DAVID KINNAMAN, BARNA GROUP

David's book is an appropriate example because it so accurately reflects the next generation's attitude toward the Christian faith. I'll say it again – the next generation is the most advertised, sold, branded, and pitched to generation in history. They see the ulterior motives from a mile away.

On the other hand, remember that the defining characteristic of the Millennial generation is that they are the most protected generation in history. Because their baby boomer parents "hovered" over them, most of these kids haven't been exposed to the real world. Being "special" is their mantra and they want to be heard. *Wall Street Journal* columnist Jeffrey Zaslow points the finger at the man who was once America's favorite next door neighbor, Mister Rogers:

You have a guy like Mister Rogers, Fred Rogers on TV. He was telling his preschoolers, "You're special. You're special." And he meant well. But we, as parents, ran with it. And we said,

"You, junior are special, and you're special and you're special and you're special." And for doing what? We didn't really explain that.

That kind of generational difference has a huge influence on the way millenials communicate, and the way we should be communicating with them.

In our own office at Cooke Pictures, our creative team was discussing this issue and made an interesting connection. We thought about the defining question of this generation: "What's on your iPod?" It's a common question in magazine interviews, on TV talk shows and in the halls of high schools across the nation. It's as if this is the one question which most accurately defines who a person really is these days. It's as if millenials believe they can assess who a person is and what they stand for based on how they answer that question. I would even venture to argue that most millennials would want to answer the "what's on your iPod" question with the following answer, "I have music from bands you've never heard of." Millenials want to discover the new, they want to start the trends – this is their unique difference.

MILLENNIALS WANT TO CREATE

A 2007 Pew Research study indicated the rapid growth of content creation among teens as they engage the conversational aspects of social media. In just three years from 2004 -2007, young people aged 12-17, engaged in content creation rose from 57 percent to 64 percent. As the study details:

> Girls continue to dominate most elements of content creation. Some 35% of all teen girls blog, compared with 20% of online boys, and 54% of wired girls post photos online compared with 40% of online boys. Boys, however, do dominate one area - posting of video content online. Online teen

boys are nearly twice as likely as online girls (19% vs. 10%) to have posted a video online somewhere where someone else could see it.

This means that a new generation not only wants to respond, but they also want to create. If the World War II generation was (as Tom Brokaw called them) "The Greatest Generation," and the Baby Boomers were the "Me Generation," perhaps the Millennials will be called the "Creative Generation."

The Pew study describes them as:

> ... a subset of teens who are super-communicators -- teens who have a host of technology options for dealing with family and friends, including traditional landline phones, cell phones, texting, social network sites, instant messaging, and email. They represent about 28% of the entire teen population and they are more likely to be older girls.

I focus on the millennials not because I'm critical of that generation – after all, it includes my children – but because that generation is our next audience. If we don't begin to understand what makes them tick, our chances of reaching them are severely diminished.

So if the typical radio preacher or TV evangelist doesn't speak to the next generation, who or what will?

This is where it gets interesting.

CHAPTER SEVEN
DESIGN IS IDENTITY:
HOW TO SPEAK TO A NEW GENERATION

> **DESIGN IS NOT JUST WHAT IT LOOKS LIKE AND FEELS LIKE. DESIGN IS HOW IT WORKS.**
>
> – STEVE JOBS, APPLE COMPUTER

In my book *Branding Faith* I discussed the often overwhelming power of design, because few things are powerful enough to unite an entire culture. Throughout history, organizations from governments to religion have tried to unite people in a variety of ways, and time after time, the choice is design. Any great study of history has to include the power of art, and from the Communist Revolution in Russia to the Civil Rights Movement in the American South, visual expression was a powerful part of sharing the story.

While teaching in Russia and Eastern Europe, I discovered that early in the life of the church, the Christian community discovered the transforming power of images. From Byzantine paintings and mosaics, to the great art of the Middle Ages and Renaissance, to the icons of Eastern Orthodoxy, the church presented it's message through the narrative storytelling of images. When peasants were illiterate, the church used *icons* – Biblical scenes beautifully painted on blocks of wood to tell the stories of Scripture.

Under Communism, Lenin exploited the visual influence of propaganda posters that were created and distributed by the millions. Kathleen and I have an original Communist era propaganda poster in our home that boasts of the growing number of movie theaters throughout the Soviet Union with Lenin's famous quote: *"Of all the arts, for us, the cinema is the greatest."*

It didn't take long for the leaders of American business to investigate the visual power of advertising; print advertising and radio and TV commercials have become their own art forms in this country. The Museum of Modern Art in New York City has a permanent collection of commercials. When the film company, owned by two partners and me, produced two TV commercials for the Super Bowl, it was as if we'd won an Academy Award.

For good or bad, since the earliest days of recorded history, the power of design has influenced millions.

Today, industrial and interior designers are the rock stars of this generation. From the intense graphic design of videogames to the pioneering special effects of major motion pictures to the storyboards of music videos and commercials and high definition television, young people today speak the language of design. Our daughters could retouch digital photos while in elementary school and by middle school our youngest, Bailey, was an accomplished photographer.

We live in a design driven world, and if the church is going to make an impact, design is the language we must learn. Take the time to notice the interior design of a typical cell phone store, coffee shop or retail mall. Compared to what most people are exposed to on a daily basis, tacky furniture, sofas, and fireplaces on Christian TV just don't cut it anymore.

And what is it about pastors and plants? Why do most sanctuary stages look like a forest?

It's time to retire four particular visual icons of the church that are tired and desperately in need of a rest:

1) Flags – There's something pastors love about the flags of the world, and I can't explain it. It began as a legitimate metaphor for reaching the nations with the gospel, but it's time for a rest. How many thousands of churches have the row of flags across the back of the sanctuary stage, or display flags hanging from the edge of the second story balcony? A symbol can be powerful, but if everyone is using it, it loses its authority. The American eagle is a great example. It's a wonderful expression of our freedom, liberty, and power, but if every other nation on the earth decided to start incorporating an eagle into their own designs, its power and impact would disappear. A symbol is most powerful and meaningful when it's unique.

2) Globes – Pretty much the same story as flags. I discovered long ago that whenever our company, Cooke Pictures, created a TV show open for a church or ministry television program, if we simply added a few globes flying around, the pastor would be thrilled beyond words. I don't know if it's about "global impact" or what, but I do know pastors and ministry leaders love globes. You find them on church stationary, business cards, signs, brochures and more. Some have been updated to modern designs but they're globes nevertheless, and since everyone's doing it, perhaps it's time for a change.

3) Flames – The fire of the Holy Spirit? The pillar of fire the Israelites followed in the desert? A consuming fire? The flames of Hell? Whatever it is, let's consider something new for your logo.

4) Doves – Sure they're in the Bible. From Noah's branch to Old Testament sacrifices to the Holy Spirit descending on Christ during his baptism, doves have a place in scripture. They often represent peace or purity. Great. Let's honor that, but find a new image for our church sign.

I talked about these issues at a pastor's conference in California and when I was finished, one of the pastors came up to the stage and said, "Phil, you've cut me to the heart." He handed me his church business card and *it had all four images on it* – a flag, globe, flames, and a dove. In fact, there were so many images on the card he had squeezed them a little too close together, and it appeared the dove had burst into flames and was crashing into the globe.

I couldn't make this stuff up.

The point? How many churches in your area use one or more of these images in their logos or advertising? Examine the images that express your church or ministry and when you do, here are some thoughts:

- **Put some real effort into your logo.** Don't let just anyone with a computer design your logo. Remember it's the first thing many people see, and if it's done right they'll remember it for a long time. Find a designer who understands what's working right now, what's contemporary, and how to use a logo to tell your brand story to the world. Secular companies spend hundreds of thousands of dollars on logo designs because they understand how a logo can impact the brand. A number of years ago I produced a promotional video presentation for a major oil company and during the editing process, three different corporate attorneys from the front office were involved just to make sure the logo was correctly presented on the screen.

- **A logo isn't a brand – it's the visual expression of the brand.** The brand is the story that surrounds you or your organization. A logo should express that story with a simple, easy to understand visual design. Does your logo visually express who you are and what you're all about? With the considerable expansion of international travel, there's been a serious shift from text-based signage to symbol-based signs. You've seen it at airports with simple stick figures that represent smoking and non-smoking areas, restrooms, baby changing rooms and more. Simplicity, clarity and lots of white space remain important elements of good design. Don't jam up your logo and try to cram everything into the design. With good design technique, you can express more with less.

- **Get expert advice.** A good designer is a critical part of the process. Don't short change expertise and real creativity. This is not a place to "be nice" and settle for less than the right person. Evaluate a designer by looking at their past work – and if your budget will allow – stretch a little and get the best you can afford.

- **Brand unity.** Once you've selected the right logo, toss the old ones out. Make sure you use that logo exclusively in all of your communication, across all media – print, web and TV. Multiple logos create a confusing brand, so make sure you're telling the same story throughout your media mix.

Living in a design culture as we do, form has become a critical key to connecting with the public.

Enough already with the criticism about moving from a text-based to a visually-based culture. Philosophers and members of the academy can discuss it, but that's just the sounds of dogs barking as the train keeps rolling. The rest of the world has moved on.

The task of future Christian media professionals will be to present a message of faith to a generation that's more visually sophisticated than any generation in history. I call it the language of this generation, and we have to realize the dramatic change that is happening right now and respond.

CHAPTER EIGHT
SHOULD WE EVER OFFEND THE AUDIENCE?
WHY CONFLICT MATTERS IN THE MEDIA

> **NEVER OFFEND PEOPLE WITH STYLE WHEN YOU CAN OFFEND THEM WITH SUBSTANCE.**
> – SAM BROWN, WASHINGTON POST, 1977

During the preparation phase of this book, it wasn't just the message of the book *UnChristian,* but both *Time Magazine* and the *Los Angeles Times* also reported the Christian faith is taking a beating in the public eye. I can relate. As I said in an earlier chapter, I grew up as a pastor's kid in the South, so I've seen every gimmick churches use to reach the public. As a Christian community we've tried entertainment, political power, criticism and boycotts, and yet we find that today, the perception of Christianity is at an all time low. The problem is we live in a media-driven culture, and most pastors and ministry leaders have no idea how to share their message in that sea of competition.

"Branding" is essentially a compelling story that surrounds a product or company, and corporate giants like Apple, Nike and Starbucks have built powerful brands that tell persuasive stories about their products. Ironically, Christianity is responsible for creating the principles we now call *branding.* For thousands of years, Christians have told compelling stories about how God changed their lives and how it can happen to others as well.

But today corporations are telling better stories. With big budgets and powerful advertising campaigns, companies like Budweiser tell better stories than many pastors. As Christians, we are rapidly losing our ability to share our story in a compelling way. As a result, the church continues to slide into cultural irrelevance.

PART OF THE CHALLENGE IS A MISPLACED BELIEF ABOUT "BEING NICE"

The history of the church is filled with preachers and Christian leaders who presented fiery, blistering messages. While I often criticize media programmers for being negative (because it is so overdone), I don't necessarily feel the same way about being provocative, angry, or satirical. After all, God has given us a wide range of emotions, and we should use them in sharing our message with the culture.

Major advertisers understand the power of emotions and aren't afraid to provoke, poke fun or be controversial. But most Christian communicators today have become fairly spineless.

Dorothy Sayers (1893-1957) was one of the famous "Inklings" – the group of writers at Oxford that included C.S. Lewis and J.R.R. Tolkien. In her book, *Letters to the Diminished Church*, she writes:

> First, I believe it to be a grave mistake to present Christianity as something charming with no offense to it. Seeing that Christ went about the world giving the most violent offense to all kinds of people, it would seem absurd to expect that the doctrine of his person can be so presented as to offend nobody. We cannot blink at the fact that gentle Jesus, meek and mild, was so stiff in his opinions and so inflammatory in his language that he was thrown out of church, stoned, hunted from place to place, and finally gibbeted as a firebrand and a public danger.

In our present day efforts not to offend, I wonder if we've taken some of the distinctiveness out of our faith. Granted, most of the people Jesus offended were the religious folks. When Jesus was confronted by sinners or those who were suffering, he was far more tender and gracious. He saved his most fiery volleys for the hypocritical types within the church.

Also, understand that when I talk about offending, I don't mean for stupid reasons. Wildly colored hair, focusing on money, Jesus junk product offers, cheesy, out of date approaches and styles, humiliating an opponent – no one has the right to be stupid in their presentation of the Christian faith. I'll fight against bad hair and tacky furniture on Christian TV until the day I die.

What I'm talking about here is presenting the honest *reality* of the Christian faith. One of the great memories I have of Billy Graham's messages is his constantly preaching, "The Bible says..." as if to say, "These aren't my rules, they come from a higher source than me."

But today, we hear pastors try everything in their arsenal to defend a point of doctrine without actually using the Scriptures. We think the audience will "relate" to it better, when it may actually be positioning the Christian faith as just another "lifestyle choice," and not the raging fire that transformed the Western world.

Are we preaching a message based on the Bible's intentions or the audience's aspirations?

Presenting the Christian faith in the media – or anywhere else for that matter – is a revolutionary act. We've lulled ourselves into thinking we have to play nice to get the audience's attention when the exact opposite is true. The most popular programs on television are provocative, funny or driven by conflict.

Let's take a moment and talk about *conflict*. Two or three times a month I have an eager young producer pitch me his or her idea for a "Christian reality show." The problem is, there's no conflict. Since the earliest days of drama, conflict has been the focal point of great writing.

The truth is, conflict is the heart of drama. In theater, television and movies, drama is driven by conflict and action. Action is anything a character does that is driven by an objective, while conflict would be more appropriately described as a clash between the motives of one or more characters.

The point is conflict is good. Conflict is what's interesting. The greatest dramatic stories are about conflict. Even the Disney movie "Bambi" has conflict. The Bible is filled with conflict. If you think about it, the greatest drama of all time is the ongoing conflict between God and Satan, between good and evil.

In its simplest form, conflict is based on the fact that the hero wants something and the villain wants to stop him.

Make sure anything you create in the media doesn't shy away from conflict. That is what keeps audiences interested and motivates great writing.

WHAT'S HAPPENED TO THE MYSTERY OF OUR FAITH? WHERE'S THE WONDER AND TRANSCENDENCE?

I'm also seeing an interesting trend among millenials that appears to be blowback from contemporary church experiences. In talking to hundreds of young people I'm hearing that in a well-intentioned effort to build churches that look more like concert arenas, we're losing our distinctiveness. Modern churches today look no different from shopping malls and theaters – but that's no different than what people experience the other 6 days of the week. Our motives were right, but I wonder, are we just duplicating the same experience you could encounter anywhere in our culture, thus making church more irrelevant?

It's tough to find mystery, wonder, and transcendence in a typical metal building mimicking the local concert arena but calling itself a church. If attending church is about the same experience as going to Disneyland, the local movie theater or shopping mall, what's the point of going? Shouldn't we be offering something that transcends those experiences?

Ultimately, the content is the most important aspect of a worship experience, and I'm not against contemporary churches or relating to people. I certainly understand budget restrictions and size limitations, but I wonder in our well-intentioned desire to embrace the culture, if we're losing the very heart of the greatest story ever told?

Are we trying so hard to be hip and contemporary, we've lost sight of the fact that the Christian faith is compelling, not because it's nice, cool or positive, but simply because it's true?

If we really believed that, it would dramatically change the way we present the Christian message.

CHAPTER NINE

CHANGE OR DIE: *IS THE LIGHT AT THE END OF THE TUNNEL THE HEADLIGHT OF AN ON-COMING TRAIN?*

> **TURBULENCE IS LIFE FORCE. IT IS OPPORTUNITY. LET'S LOVE TURBULENCE AND USE IT FOR CHANGE.**
>
> – RAMSAY CLARK

The Hollywood writer's strike in 2007 and 2008 was much more than a typical labor negotiation. The strike was motivated by the debate over royalties on digital media – particularly when movies and other entertainment projects are released online. At the time, and from the studio's perspective, the digital media universe was uncharted territory. Steve Jobs with Apple's iTunes was one of the few who actually figured out how to make money with entertainment on the Internet. Hundreds of millions of investor dollars have been lost on failed attempts at various other online money making ventures.

At the same time, writers were still stinging from the last major negotiation with studios, when the sticking point was video and DVD royalties. Back in those days, video and DVD sales were a new domain, and as a result, the writers settled for far less than they feel they should have. As a result, the maker of a DVD package was often making more from the DVD release of a movie than the man or woman who wrote the film, or created the original idea.

The strike also peeled back and exposed radical changes happening in the media business, and particularly for faith-based communicators, we have a rare chance to understand the change and prepare for the transition. It doesn't take a media genius to see that we're at a dramatic crossroads in the global media business, and as in the past, religious broadcasting is not immune.

This change is so important that I believe many in our industry will lose their station, network, or ministry in coming years because they don't recognize the light at the end of the tunnel is the actually the headlight of an oncoming train.

But others will recognize the crossroads, make the appropriate adjustments (although some may be painful), and in so doing, respond to a changing culture. As a media strategist working with faith-based program producers, I've encountered four key areas of change that will impact us most during the next few years:

1) The Importance of Branding and Identity
As I've mentioned, researchers tell us that we're being overwhelmed with more than 3,000 – 5,000 advertising messages per day. The typical family now watches TV and surfs the web nearly six hours a day, and by the time the average teen is eighteen years old, they've already seen 100,000 beer commercials alone. The Census Bureau reported that in 2008, the average young person spent 5½ months watching TV, movies, surfing the Internet, or listening to their digital music player.

On November 25, 2008, the Nielsen rating service released the news that television use is now at an all time high in the United States. In a typical home, the TV is now turned on for 8 hours and 18 minutes per day, and is actually being viewed more than 4 of those hours. By comparison, the average American gets only 6 hours, 40 minutes of sleep every night according to a poll by the National Sleep Foundation. It's also worth noting that more and more TV is being *time-shifted*. Nielsen reports that 6 and a half hours a month are being viewed at other times from their original broadcast from digital video recorders, which are now in 27% of homes. Susan Whiting, vice-chairwoman for Nielsen said that "TV remains the dominant choice for most Americans, yet time-shifting as well as videos on the Internet and on mobile phones continue to be trends to watch."

A revolution is indeed happening.

The media clutter in our lives has become a tidal wave, and few are equipped to deal with the impact media is having the world.

That's why branding is so important. In my book, *Branding Faith: Why Some Churches and Non-Profits Impact the Culture and Others Don't*, I discuss how to share your message in a media-driven culture. It's about choice and how to get your message heard amid the crushing media clutter that bombards our lives. When my grandmother went to the local general store in North Carolina back the 1920's, there was only one brand of sugar, one brand of flour, and one brand of salt. Today, the average grocery store in America stocks as many as 30,000 items. There are eight or more different types of Oreo cookies alone!

In the same way, radio and TV programs, Internet sites, movies and digital media have created an overwhelming number of choices for the average media consumer. So just as companies like Apple, Nike and Starbucks have built unique and original identities to make their products stand out from the pack, our churches and media programming must do the same. The optimum questions are:

- What do people think of when they think of you, your program or your organization?
- What's the brand story that surrounds you or your program?
- What makes you or your program unique and different?

To avoid getting your message lost in the swirl of our media-driven culture, your message must be original, unique and innovative. Ultimately, it's about how the audience, congregation or donors perceive you and your story. It's worth re-stating that in a media-driven environment, how you're perceived is just as important as who you are. If you don't begin to control your perception, you'll spend the rest of your life at the mercy of others who will.

2) The Digital Age Is the "Wild West"

The digital world is changing everything we know and understand about the media. I've already predicted that this decade will be remembered as the era that killed mass media, because the future is *customized* media. In years past, radio and TV programmers had the luxury of creating what they believed the audience wanted. Audiences had little choice, and as a result, yesterday's audiences took what programmers were dishing out.

That's all changed and today the audience is in charge. I rarely listen to the radio anymore, because on my iPod, I can create my own playlists. I can design the music rotation, listen to the podcasts of my choice or hear the teaching programs I choose, when I want to hear them. With the development of digital recorders like TIVO, it's no different with television. I watch TV on my terms now. If you think you're in charge of what your viewers and listeners want and when they want it – think again.

A 2008 Pew Research report showed that 55 percent of all adult Americans now have a high-speed internet connection at home. The percentage of Americans with broadband at home has grown from 47 percent in early 2007. Nearly one-third of broadband users pay extra to get faster connections.

Change is happening out there, and it's happening fast.

Don't simply charge headlong into the technology frenzy – strategy is critical. For instance, while many predict that the future of TV is the cell phone, I'm convinced that's as lame a prediction as those who were preparing for the demise of radio after the invention of television. Remember – it's about choice. While there are plenty of entertainment functions for my cell phone, the Super Bowl isn't one of them. There will always be things I prefer to watch on my big HD plasma screen TV.

So the key factors of the technological battle are choice, usability and need. Just because technology allows me to receive devotional messages on my cell phone doesn't mean I want them. But Google alerts on my cell phone telling me my plane is late? That is a miracle!

Don't for a minute believe you're locked into radio or TV to start a successful media ministry anymore. Pastors like Mark Crow in Oklahoma City have successful online TV networks with significant audiences. Pastors Erwin McManus and Rob Bell produce short films. Biola University graduate Josh Sikora wanted to become a Hollywood film director, but he knew it would take at least 10 years for that to happen. Understanding that in 10 years, Hollywood as we know it might not exist, he created Web Serials (webserials.com) which produces serialized dramatic feature films for Internet consumption. He's become so successful that he's now a content partner with YouTube. This young director, only a few years out of college, may help change the way we look at movies in the future.

As I write this, a new website, "SnagFilms," just launched as a vehicle to distribute documentary films online. By using a simple widget, anyone can offer full length feature documentaries through their own websites. SnagFilms has access to a growing library of independent documentaries, and now anyone with a blog, website, or social networking page can be a veritable mobile movie theater.

When you click on the widget and select a movie, SnagFilms shows a short advertisement at the beginning of the presentation. While the website owner doesn't receive any revenue, the advertiser pays a fee that's split between the movie producer and SnagFilms.

It's a great idea for getting documentary films in front of a new audience, and an even better idea of how innovative thinking is using the web to change media distribution for the better.

When it comes to technology, stop thinking "outside the box" because *there is no longer a box.* The digital universe is the wild West and the next generation pioneers will determine what happens next.

3) Generational Change

I believe Christian media is facing the greatest generational transition in the history of our industry. For the most part, the first generation pioneers like Billy Graham, Oral Roberts, Jerry Falwell, James Dobson, D. James Kennedy, Robert Schuller, Pat Robertson and Paul Crouch have either passed away, retired, or are no longer as intensely involved in their ministries as they used to be. I've had the opportunity to be involved in numerous transitions from a variety of first generation to second generation leaders. Those transitions run the gamut from easy successions to not so easy and in some cases, so difficult attorneys, contracts, and difficult negotiations were necessary. You'd be shocked by some of the stories of such transitions.

However, this is an important and relevant topic because some of the largest and most influential religious media organizations have recently been through a transition or will be going through one soon. The implications of these transitions are more critical than many might believe. For instance:

- **It means a transition in leadership styles.** First generation leaders are often more creative, driven and relentless. They are founders, and the incredible energy and passion it takes to create "lift-off" for an organization leaves little time for anything else. As a result, most first generation leaders don't value teamwork, they have charismatic personalities that inspire great loyalty (sometimes with egos to match), and laser focus – sometimes at the expense of their own families. They know what they want, when they want it, and how they want it delivered. They are specific. As a result, their influence lives on, long after they've left the day-to-day operation. In fact, if the second generation leader isn't strong enough to assert his or her authority and style, he or she could spend their years implementing the founder's vision rather than their own.

By contrast, most second generation leaders are more comfortable with technology, value teamwork, and legislate through consensus. They tend to be less driven, and rather than pushing so hard to create the organization, they are able to re-focus management on expansion or new markets.

There are pluses and minuses to both styles, but because of the dramatic difference, organizations that are experiencing generational change often convulse under the stress. Managers and employees suddenly have to switch gears, adjust expectations and change their thinking. Those that recognize the change adapt quickly, but others, stumble and often fail.

- **The move from a personality-driven ministry to an institutional style of ministry.** The first generation of Christian media leaders, in many cases, ran personality-driven ministries. Largely, because pastors and evangelists were the first to seize on the opportunities in radio and TV early in the last century, they raised up organizations built around their personalities. But with the passing of that personality, some organizations are confronted with the need to change to a more corporate vision, where everything does not hinge on a single person.

  That transition has huge implications for the brand, program structure, fundraising, and management, but it can be done successfully. Organizations like The American Bible Society, World Vision and others have proven a broader corporate structure works. How well many major personality-driven organizations will make that transition is yet to be seen.

- **It means changing the way we impact the culture.** Think about the first generation of Christian media leaders. By and large these were brilliant men and women who were confronted with the incredible cultural tumult that began in the 1960s.

Their first reaction? Confrontation. It was a logical choice given the timing and background of their ministries. The societal changes taking place early in their ministries were shocking, and they reacted logically – they confronted the problem. They complained, protested and often boycotted in a well-intentioned effort to hold back the tide they felt was destroying the culture.

But today, a new generation of leaders has grown up living with the cultural and moral changes that began decades ago. The only culture they know is one full of violent and sexually explicit entertainment, hostility toward religious faith, crumbling morality and disintegrating families. They have more experience navigating that world.

As a result, when a movie like "The Da Vinci Code" hits theaters, the first generation leaders were more prone to criticize or boycott, and the second generation leaders were more prone to use it as a platform for sharing their faith.

When I spoke out about the movie before its premiere, I didn't call for *boycotts*, I called for *engagement*. After all, just get on a plane with a copy of "The Da Vinci Code" in your lap and someone will ask you about it.

What a great platform for sharing the real story.

In fact, I was a guest on Paula Zahn's program on CNN to discuss the film and I discovered at the last minute they had positioned me against a very conservative national ministry leader. He was angry to say the least. He was calling for a boycott, or at the very least a disclaimer at the front of the movie saying that the story wasn't based on true facts or church doctrine.

First, I realized that a national boycott would only draw more people to the film, and second, if we could successfully tack a disclaimer on *this* film, non-believers could do the same for films like "The Passion of the Christ." I tried to discuss the issues, but he just wouldn't hear it. He already had an agenda, and he was all about anger, hatred and bitterness. Once he expanded the discussion to derogatory comments about other subjects I had to step in.

In the middle of the interview, I bluntly asked him, "Tell me, how does embarrassment, shame, and humiliation work for you as a tool for evangelism? How many people have you brought to Christ because you embarrassed or shamed them into it?"

He shut up and didn't say another word during the entire interview. As a media strategist, I never rule out boycotts, but I view them as a "nuclear option" – to be used as a last resort. On the other hand, as a producer working in Hollywood, I see first hand the impact of *engagement*. Today, major studios have faith-based film divisions, and I've personally been invited to talk with some of them to help them understand who the faith-based audience is, and what they're looking for from the entertainment world. Had I criticized or boycotted them, they would have never been interested in having that conversation.

4) Fundraising Is Changing

This is true both with religious organizations and secular non-profits. Generally speaking, for the last generation, when people gave they wanted to be noticed. That's why your local church fellowship hall, medical center, library, or university dorm is named after someone. How many Christian radio or TV stations in America have a painting of a tree in the lobby with donors names on the leaves, or bricks at the entrance with donor names engraved on them?

Ministries gave these donors a "gift" in return for their do- nation, and in the process, created an audience who "gives to get." I don't think it's a coincidence that "seed faith" was in- vented about the same time Christian TV was born. Faced with the staggering costs of the medium at that time, having people realize they could get blessed with a financial miracle just made it easier to give.

Today we're dealing with a generation that tends to give, not to be noticed, but because it is the right thing to do. Major global needs like hunger, poverty and environmental issues are hard to ignore these days and the younger generation under- stand the importance of making a difference. We have yet to notice a trend, but early on, I'm finding that many givers today don't need to have their name engraved on a brick or receive a trinket in the mail. Hopefully, that means the unending ava- lanche of "Jesus Junk" product offers is on the decline.

That's not to say that motivating the younger generation to give will be easy. There is no question, driving millenials to give to Chris- tian causes will be a challenge.

We've been blessed over the last 40 years with Christians who were trained to give to ministry causes, and who have donated hundreds of millions to make evangelism, disciple- ship and relief work possible around the world. Inspiring a new generation to pick up where the other left off will be a real challenge.

For the record, I'm not against fundraising. Truth be told, I'm frustrated that more Christians don't do a better and more consistent job of giving. The fundraising landscape is changing, and only those organizations experimenting with new methods and ideas will be in a position to discover what will work with the next generation.

The key to being effective will be creating a strong brand in the media marketplace, understanding how strategy impacts digital technology, managing smooth leadership transitions, and staying connected to your donors. It's about presenting a compelling vision, and telling a story that can impact a generation.

EVERY GENERATION COMMUNICATES DIFFERENTLY

For my parents, the telephone was a revolution. In the rural South, where mom and dad grew up, "party lines" where shared phone systems where people had to take turns. And yes, you could listen to everyone else's conversation. In those days privacy wasn't an issue because nobody had any.

For me, the revolution was *electronic mail*. I was an early adopter, and I remember carrying around a tool kit during trips so I could dismantle the phone jack in hotel rooms, hook up my computer and email. Today, I have a cell card on my laptop so I can receive email just about anywhere in the world or I can access it on my iPhone. I thought I was the Jedi Knight of email, until I heard author Leonard Sweet describe it as simply, " an electronic version of a traditional letter."

Once I thought about it, I realized he was right. An email message is addressed to one or more people, you write it much like a normal letter, include an email signature and push send. It's an electronic embodiment of a traditional paper letter and when you look at it that way, with the exception of speed, it's a relatively small leap from a functional perspective.

My daughters on the other hand rarely use email at all. They're "instant message" people, and can be involved in as many as 10 different IM conversations simultaneously. The concept of a letter – email or otherwise – is almost foreign to them. And now with Twitter and other mobile messaging programs, it's likely that within another generation email will be something we tell our grandkids about.

The point is that generations communicate differently and as we address different generations, we need to be ready for that kind of diversity. Do we stop our traditional direct mail or phone outreach to donors? Absolutely not. That's precisely the way that particular generation prefers to communicate. But we can't limit ourselves to using only those methods. We have to be open to letting our donors dictate the method of communication they prefer and following suit – because if we fail there, the conversation will never begin.

WHERE A CALCULATOR ON THE ENIAC IS EQUIPPED WITH 18,000 VACUUM TUBES AND WEIGHS 30 TONS, COMPUTERS IN THE FUTURE MAY HAVE ONLY 1,000 VACUUM TUBES AND PERHAPS WEIGH 1.5 TONS.

– POPULAR MECHANICS MAGAZINE, MARCH 1949

I've criticized what others are doing, so what's my solution, you ask? Here's where it gets not only interesting but also mysterious, frustrating, infuriating and fun. The "new" is always uncharted territory, and as the above quote illustrates – not all prophecies are quite accurate.

But we don't need a prophetic gift when it comes to predicting the future of media. In Matthew 16, Jesus was upset with the religious leaders of his day because they could interpret the appearance of the sky but were unable (or refused) to read the signs of the times. In the same way, there are digital signposts today that indicate the direction our culture is moving and how to engage with them and communicate a message of hope.

The only condition is that we have to be looking and listening. Far too many communicators today have already decided what they want to say and how they want to say it. In the process, they've stopped listening to the culture and watching how trends work. They've become closed off from a vibrant connection with the very people they are trying to reach and as a result, have lost the interest of the audience.

I received a call recently from a pastor who wanted to launch a new television program within 90 days. When I asked him about the rush, he told me a media buyer had found a really good timeslot on a local television program, and he wanted to take advantage of the deal. Aside from the enormous *engineering* challenge of pulling off the lighting, video equipment, and other technical and production considerations within three months, the pastor had not even begun to think about how to reach the right audience, the content or style of the program, or any other question of content, creativity or media strategy.

That kind of shallow thinking about creating a media ministry is crippling much of religious media today.

So where *should* we start?

INFLUENCE THE INFLUENCERS

One of the reasons the message of the early church spread is because many of the earliest believers worked in Roman households. They may not have held positions of great authority, but they worked side by side in the homes and businesses of those who did. They were trusted. They listened. And as a result, they often had the ability to influence the people who had the power to influence the culture of the time.

We start engaging the culture by listening.

I had to pause writing this chapter because I was interviewed by a national business magazine for a feature story about one of our biggest clients, a church led by a pastor who is extremely popular. The editors of the business magazine were amazed at how well this pastor's organization is managed. As the person behind the branding, he wanted to talk with me about how churches today are hitting or missing the mark when it comes to engaging the culture. As I talked with him, I realized that this writer of a national business magazine based in New York City noticed the church, not because of their *message*, but of its *excellence and expertise*. Because of that excellence, he was pulled into the message.

The culture respects expertise and when I began working with that particular client, we understood that if we created a media ministry that reflected state of the art excellence, it would be noticed. That phone call confirmed we were right. To connect with today's world, it is vitally important to listen to the culture and respond accordingly.

Right now, the entertainment and media industries are going through the most nerve-wracking, unsure and remarkable change in history. Major companies are putting millions on the line to create a media platform for future consumers and everyone from a local church in the Midwest to the major Hollywood studios are trying to piece together a strategic best guess about how to reach tomorrow's audience.

To me, one of the most remarkable trends is the blurring of traditional media lines. Ideas that were unheard of just a few years ago are now becoming almost commonplace:

- Sherwood Baptist Church in Georgia, the makers of the movies, "Facing the Giants" and "Fireproof," signed a output deal to make movies with a major Hollywood studio
- A young director is a content partner with YouTube, just one year after graduating from a Christian college
- Major studios now have faith-based film divisions
- American Idol recently closed a special event program with, "Shout to the Lord," a popular worship song
- Teenagers from church youth groups create amateur videos for YouTube that reach thousands of viewers
- A young mom hosts a blog that generates $40,000 a month in advertising revenue
- Film festivals that celebrate faith are receiving record submissions

- TV commercials are evolving to become "branded entertainment," and increasingly, the spots are more engaging than the programming they sponsor

What, a generation ago, was the realm of Hollywood studios or global media companies exclusively, is now within the reach of any high school kid with Internet access. These days political campaigns are influenced by bloggers as much as the national news organizations.

It's worth noting that the blogging world also includes voices who are not only incompetent, but in many cases, downright nuts. Because anyone with an idea (no matter how strange) can download inexpensive blogging software, there are some wacky things being said online. Writer Andrew Keen, author of *The Cult of the Amateur: How blogs, MySpace, YouTube, and the rest of today's user-generated media are destroying our economy, our culture, and our values*, points out that there's no substitute for professionally trained writers and journalists. While I don't agree that user-generated media heralds the demise of civilization, there's no question that we must be careful with what we believe online.

SHIFT HAPPENS

The influence has shifted and we need to respond. We're already seeing it in the giving patterns of traditional media ministries. While most organizations would say they don't have hard data to back up this assertion, I can tell you from personal experience, there's real sweating going on in many planning meetings at major churches, ministries, and nonprofit organizations these days.

The future of direct mail fundraising is even in transition. Will it entirely go away anytime soon? No, but with the rising cost of postage, paper and the manpower to create direct mail campaigns, most ministry organizations are beginning a slow but purposeful shift to online fundraising.

If you want a vision of the future of ministry and non-profit fundraising, study how political candidates are successfully doing it online *right now*.

And speaking of change, just a quick look at how consumer media use changed between 2001 and 2006 is an eye-opening revelation. According to a combined study from Veronis Suhler Stevenson, PQ Media, Adams Media Research, Alexander & Associates, Arbitron, Audit Bureau of Circulations, Ball State University Media Design Center, and Booz Allen Analysis, the shift indicates the following:

MEDIA MIGRATION (HOURS PER YEAR)

MUSIC	-18%
BROADCAST TV	-13%
NEWSPAPERS	-11%
MAGAZINES	-5%
THEATRICAL MOVIES	-3%
RADIO	-2%
VIDEOGAMES	+15%
CABLE AND SATTELITE	+28%
HOME VIDEO	+31%
INTERNET	+41%
MOBILE	+1264%

While these developments don't necessarily mean the demise of traditional media ministries or methods, something significant is going on. From my perspective, that "something" is the sound of new voices. People who realize a shift is happening and are responding to that change with more relevant content distributed on more contemporary platforms in far more compelling ways.

A 2008 Frank N. Magid Associates survey published in *USA Today* revealed what people are watching online:

> 37% - *Comedy, jokes, bloopers*
> 36% - *Music videos*
> 33% - *Clips on video-sharing sites*
> 31% - *News stories*
> 28% - *Movie previews*

To me it seems clear that a single medium is no longer enough to capture the full attention of a consumer. As more media options become available, rather than eliminating previous media choices, new choices are simply added to the mix. We call it "media multitasking" and anyone with a teenager in the house understands exactly what I'm talking about. After all, children don't toss out older toys when you buy new ones, they just add the new ones to the toy box.

And it's not just about kids. Statistics indicate that 66 percent of TV viewers are online *at the same time* they watch TV, while 59 percent of people watch TV while reading a magazine.

With that in mind, here's a list of some of the most significant changes happening in religious media today, and where we're headed:

1) "IPTV" – Internet Protocol Television
IPTV represents the shift from traditional broadcast television to the web. While the formats and platforms are still in flux, there's no question that convergence is happening. At the time of this writing, major players like Joost, Hulu, and abc.com are battling for online viewers and new channels and networks are springing up almost daily.

One of the most prominent players in the religious media world right now is Sky Angel (skyangel.com), a multiple channel TV and radio service that shifted completely from satellite broadcasting to IPTV in 2008. Sky Angel isn't a single channel, but an aggregate platform that offers as many as 30 religious TV and radio channels as well as multiple family channels like Discovery, History, Animal Planet and others. With a small, portable set-top box, you can take your TV channels anywhere in the world as long as you can access a high-speed Internet connection.

Tom Scott, president and chief operating officer of Sky Angel put it this way:

> Sky Angel is on the cutting edge of Christian media of the future. Churches will undoubtedly continue to utilize media to maintain and expand their role in the community. Technology will increasingly allow church members to engage in a worship experience outside the physical confines of the church. Will a generation weaned on HD, Wi Fi, text messaging, Play Stations, MP3's and mobile delivery of content, continue to be attracted to traditional "pew and preach" experiences? If the church fails to address this issue and the role of technology in providing a solution, there may be far reaching implications on its ability to maintain church rolls and communication with its members. It is no longer open to dispute that media will be an increasingly vital part of church ministry.

With technological advances in buffering and video distribution, the quality of IPTV is remarkable. Several services like Joost and Hulu even offer their channels directly through the web without an external box.

Some churches are already programming their own IPTV channels that can be accessed through their websites. Using their libraries of videotaped sermons, teaching materials, music, worship, concerts, skits and music videos they're creating 24/7 channels accessible online, anywhere in the world.

In chapter nine, I mentioned Joshua Sikora, a recent Biola University graduate who created webserials.com and with zero budget, he and a group of friends began shooting feature films on digital video in short serialized segments. Each week, they upload a new 5-10 minute segment, and he's developed such a large and loyal audience that YouTube has made him a content partner. Once he's uploaded all the individual serialized episodes, his team will then edit them into a complete feature and sell the movie online. Ten years ago, to reach the number of viewers webserials.com is reaching today would have cost millions.

Advertisers have discovered online video and it's changing the way we market products and companies. Years ago, when bmw.com hired a group of hot Hollywood feature directors to create a series of short, online films focused around BMW automobiles, it was the leading edge of what companies are now doing every day. New product introductions, tie-ins with television commercial campaigns, deeper background on products, teaching and training are all ways agencies are exposing the public to their clients' products.

Many of these companies release their short films on the Internet with no fanfare and let the viral nature of the web take over. Recently, a major automobile company produced a documentary where their car played only a peripheral part of the movie. They posted it online without telling anyone it was sponsored and the viewers assumed it was created by an independent producer. Hundreds of thousands of people watched the film before the company finally confessed and admitted they produced the movie.

"The Cult of Sincerity" is an online movie created by a group of young, innovative thinkers and a very small budget. Rather than taking a long shot on a theatrical or TV release, they distributed their independent film via YouTube, but first, they made a deal with a music downloading company. They promoted the music company at the front of the movie, and then anytime a viewer went to the music company's website and registered, the company would contribute to the cost of the film.

In just the first weekend of the film's release online, the music company paid for 10 percent of the movie's budget.

The uploading frenzy for movies and short films is so great, Internet companies are wondering about the ability of the current web infrastructure to handle the explosion in bandwidth. And with IPTV and other media distribution channels, change continues. Chances are, by the time you read this book, many of my examples will outdated – bought out by bigger companies or gone out of business. The model is in flux, it is changing everyday and even the major players haven't yet sorted out the playing field.

Right now, the digital media world isn't about income, it's about influence.

While traditional media still makes the money and wields the power, a significant new paradigm is emerging – and it's all about immediacy and connection.

Television may be the king of now, but digital media is the king of tomorrow.

If you're waiting for digital media to become cost-effective, you're already being left behind. While traditional media is concerned about *making money*, the new digital pioneers are concerned about *change*.

2) The Rise of Social Media

Possibly the greatest phenomenon of the last decade is the popularity and power of social media. Websites like Facebook and Myspace have generated hundreds of millions of users, and few people under 30 today don't have a personal page on either – or both – sites. These vast social networks offer people new ways to meet, interact and exchange information.

In many ways social networking is the new office water cooler, just on an exponentially larger scale.

Similar sites like LinkedIn assist in the networking of business people and encourage building relationships and alliances in the workplace. The concept has become so popular, software developers are moving from creating stand alone programs to plug-in applications for social networking sites. It's creating a massive shift in the entire principle of software creation and implementation.

From a Christian perspective, GodTube (godtube.com), an extremely popular video sharing site focused on Christian videos, is going through major re-branding and structuring and is scheduled to re-launch about the time of the release of this book in January 2009. The new site will be called "Tangle," (think "intertwining social networks" or "I am the vine and you are the branches") and the plans are for it to expand into a MySpace/Facebook hybrid. It will encompass options for home pages for individuals, ministries, churches groups, bands and artists, and expand to include discussion forums, podcasting, as well as a new interactive virtual bible that will allow for sharing, tagging, and commenting on individual verses. The video sharing section of GodTube will still be a key part of the new Tangle.

I don't need to give you the background on this cultural trend, because if you don't know what I'm talking about, you've apparently been living on another planet. Let me mention a few things I find particularly interesting about social media platforms:

1) It has changed the way a generation interacts. Many young people today enjoy their *digital* space as much as their *people* space. Simply put, they'd rather send you a text message or email than talk to you face to face. The teenage daughter of a friend of mine sent out 2,500 text messages in a single month. That's about 85 per day. Aside from the cell phone bill, my first question was how is that even possible? How do you have the time?

Is it a problem? We don't know yet, but we need to understand the ramifications of a generation raised connecting through the web. One young person asked me the other day, "How in the world did you meet friends in college without Facebook?"

She was serious.

2) It's changing the traditional workplace paradigm. On the one hand, social networking online means that employers are facing a significant loss of control over workers. The traditional picture of the pyramid top-down style of management has been blown asunder, as employees can now connect with other companies, fritter their day away on YouTube, leak company secrets through email or criticize management in a public manner.

On the other hand, it has released *motivated* employees to make their own deals, expand the company's influence and rapidly expand their sales and networking contacts. In some ways, the actual working structure of companies has been changed, as particularly motivated employees migrate together to work on specific projects, with or without the approval of upper management. Once employees connect online, the old traditional department/manager/employee paradigm actually means very little.

Whatever the potential, in my view, it will dramatically change the dynamics in the workplace – both for better and for worse.

3) That much time using technology may have consequences. According to the *Los Angeles Times*, a Korean study on cell phone usage discovered what may be a correlation between growing cell phone use and rising rates of depression among young people. It's too early for a definitive judgment, but in that country, where teenagers make as many as 90 or more cell phone calls a day, it is worth watching.

4) Exposing your life on the web has a downside. I'm seeing an interesting conflict as twenty-somethings leave college and start looking for a full-time jobs. Remember, this is a generation that grew up revealing the most intimate details of their lives on their Myspace or Facebook pages; pictures of getting drunk in Cabo, fooling around on spring break or other goofy stuff is the status quo on many profile pages.

What these young people don't realize is as soon as they leave a job interview – or in many cases before they even get an interview – the first thing a prospective employer does is Google them. And guess what comes up?

> **SOCIAL NETWORKING SITES ARE JUST ANOTHER WAY THAT PEOPLE SAY AND DO THINGS THAT COME BACK AND HAUNT THEM. THE THINGS THAT PEOPLE SAY ONLINE OR LEAVE ONLINE ARE PRETTY PERMANENT.**
> – PHIL MALONE, DIRECTOR OF THE CYBERLAW CLINIC, HARVARD LAW SCHOOL

Online Photos Can Sting.
Thousands of kids are finding it difficult to convince employers of their maturity after a cursory glance at their Myspace pages. I was in Miami recently and listened to a statewide public service radio campaign attempting to discourage young women from posting suggestive or explicitly sexual photos on their websites. The spot made clear that once it's posted, the photos can easily be copied, redistributed and viewed by pedophiles, stalkers, the leering neighbor next door, or perhaps most embarrassing of all, their parents.

In 2008 the *Associated Press* reported that prosecutors have begun using photos posted on social networking sites to embarrass and damage the reputation of defendants.

In one case the AP reported that a 20-year old college junior was arrested for a drunk driving crash that seriously injured another driver. At the trial, prosecutors displayed photos the young man had posted on his Facebook page at a party showing him drunk and dressed in an orange county prison uniform with "jailbird" stamped on the shirt. Although the photos had nothing directly to do with the case at hand, they were used to paint the defendant as an unrepentant partier who was living it up while his victim suffered in the hospital.

The false sense of "privacy" online has invaded adult life as well. I recently helped a church get through a difficult crisis with the media when a member of their pastoral staff was arrested for soliciting sex with a minor. Apparently the middle aged associate pastor (and grandfather) had been having an online conversation with someone he *thought* was a 13-year-old girl, when in fact it was an undercover police officer. Needless to say, he was arrested after a three hour drive on his way to a rendezvous.

More interesting to *this* conversation was the revelation that when the police found his social networking page he had apparently been having multiple conversations with actual minors. Keep in mind that this was a member of the pastoral staff of a large church in a major metropolitan area, who felt comfortable having explicit conversations with minors on a social networking site – a site that is a *public* platform.

There is a strange mental shift taking place; When people post to a social networking site – which is available to millions of viewers – they still feel that it is somehow a private space. We have yet to see or imagine the social implications as this phenomenon develops.

SOCIAL NETWORKING FOR A CAUSE

Social networks are also providing a platform for private companies and non-profits. Some online communities aggregate important causes and encourage giving through a single portal for a variety of needs. Sites like sixdegrees.org, realitycharity. org, givemeaning.org and justgive.org are all secular sites that encourage donations and/or personal involvement to a wide variety of projects and causes.

From a slightly different perspective, companies, non-profits and even churches are creating online communities for their members, but it's important to realize that the online behavior of these "insider" communities is often dramatically different from public sites like Myspace and Facebook.

The company "Communispace" has created more than 250 online communities for major companies like Hilton, Capitol One, Pepsi and General Mills and recently researched the behavior of more than 26,500 members of 66 online communities. As reported in Christopher Vollmer's book, *Always On*, they discovered some interesting principles to consider when creating social networks:

1) Intimacy breeds participation: 86 percent of people who logged on were active contributors. Only 14 percent "lurked." On public social sites like Facebook those numbers are reversed. This suggests the more intimate and comfortable the setting, the more people want to be actively involved. If you create an "insider" group, make sure it is totally focused on a particular, niche audience.

2) Familiarity is a powerful driver: Branded sites had the highest volume of participation.

3) Men and women respond differently: In the research, more women participated than men, but when men participated they logged on with more frequency.

4) Homogeneity triggers participation: Communities built around specific demographics saw increased participation. For instance, social networks built around gender or ethnic lines had more participation than more general, all-inclusive sites.

One of the most exciting aspects of social networks for individual companies, organizations and churches is the access to a wealth of consumer data. Through chat rooms, online surveys, discussion threads, polls and more, companies, organizations and churches can mine enormous amounts of information about the behavior, tastes and preferences of their target audiences.

THE VIRTUAL UNIVERSE

Beyond social networks would be virtual worlds like *Second Life*. What began with fantasy games like "World of Warcraft" (with 9 million subscribers worldwide as of July 2007) has evolved into virtual societies like Second Life, known for having its own currency and community structures. While advertisers initially made significant inroads into virtual communities, the jury is out on whether or not it is an effective marketing strategy.

In the faith-based arena, pastor Craig Groeschel's LifeChurch.tv has created a virtual church experience within Second Life. When I asked the church's innovation leader Bobby Gruenewald about his vision for the Second Life project, he (appropriately) directed me to comments from his blog:

> The good news is that Second Life is just one of a growing number of companies building 3-D virtual worlds (aka metaverses). Now… I am not interested in building private 3-D "club houses" for Christians since I am focused on using these tools to reach people who are not followers of Christ. I do, however, think there are ways to use a platform like this to build 3-D environments (even games) that can engage people who would never step foot in a church otherwise.

3) Filmmaking

Another explosive area of growth is the production of independent – especially *short* films. Today most major Christian colleges and universities have media departments, and some even boast serious film festivals. Biola University and Fuller Seminary take groups of students to the Sundance Film Festival each year in Park City, Utah. In addition, short film festivals like the 168 Hour Film Festival, Heartland or the Damah Festival encourage the production of hundreds of short films that explore themes of faith and spirituality.

Pastors like Rob Bell and Erwin McManus are creating shorts, and as I mentioned before, the "Crave" short film series hosted by Erwin is being distributed by a major Hollywood studio. This generation is attracted by short films as a way to tell a compelling story on a limited budget. I'm also seeing local churches using short films in their services and on their websites.

George and Daniel Temple at Sermon Spice (sermonspice. com) are currently the largest suppliers of short films and videos to pastors today. The Sermon Spice website lists a vast library of short films on a wide variety of subjects that a local pastor can download and use during a service. Of course even technology can't change certain habits. The busiest time for downloading for Sermon Spice videos? *Saturday night.*

Apparently, when it comes to sermon preparation, some things never change.

Because of their innovative revenue sharing arrangement, Sermon Spice has built a loyal army of filmmakers creating Christian content. As of this writing, the company is receiving more than 100 short films submissions every week. Now, a church media director in Omaha who would normally produce a short video for his church, knows that if he can increase the production value, he could also submit it to Sermon Spice (or similar sites) and not only eventually pay for the production, but potentially make a profit. That's great encouragement and motivation for thousands of young filmmakers across the country.

Who knows? Over the next five to ten years, digital media sites like Sermon Spice may do more to help the church realize the power of creative filmmaking – and eventually impact the entertainment industry – than all the film schools at all the Christian colleges combined.

4) Cause Marketing

"Cause marketing" is what corporations call their support of important social causes. Global hunger, human trafficking, poverty and disaster relief are some of the causes major corporations are addressing today. For the most part, these are humanitarian projects supported by secular companies, but they are critically important because they often tackle extremely large, high-profile projects.

Rock stars like U2's Bono often are headliners for such campaigns and they will often partner with corporations such as American Express. The best brands know how to transform products into lifestyles. Signing up for a hunger campaign led by Bono not only allows you to address the problem by giving, but it also gives you an insider's look to the rock star driven world of entertainment.

The Whole Foods grocery chain is a perfect example. Buying at Whole Foods is a good idea because they sell organic, healthy food. But as Kathleen and I watch people walking through the Los Angeles store, we can also see they feel they are part of a movement. Through innovative positioning that connects certain Whole Foods products to fair trade, anti-poverty and global warming campaigns, Whole Foods customers feel like they are getting more than quality products, they feel part of a lifestyle.

Some have questioned the motives of many of these companies, and I must admit I've seen many companies move these projects from their charitable giving departments or foundations to their marketing departments.

Companies have discovered that supporting charities can be good for business.

On the surface I couldn't be happier, but upon closer inspection I find that many companies are supporting charities for all the wrong reasons. Motivation still matters. One popular book on the subject is subtitled, *"Results-Oriented* Cause Marketing," indicating the positive marketing buzz available for companies who are perceived as being charitable and how they can profit from giving. Does this make corporate support for important causes suspect? Not necessarily. But it's important to be aware of why companies give. Hopefully they're doing it for the right reasons and not just to garner positive PR. On the other hand, giving is giving, and regardless of the motivation, attempts to eradicate problems like HIV or poverty are a good thing.

WHY A NEW GENERATION IS ATTRACTED TO CAUSE MARKETING

The most important issue to consider in regards to cause marketing is how and why a younger generation is attracted to the idea. Today, plenty of Christian media organizations are feeding the poor, helping end poverty or human trafficking, but younger audiences are more likely to be drawn to a similar – though purely secular – effort because of the celebrity names, the creative branding or the perceived "hip" factor.

That doesn't mean we should shift our charitable work to issues that happen to be "hot" in the culture. But it is important to examine what is attractive about some of these efforts and see if elements can be applied to your project or ministry.

Because there is so much competition for donor dollars, today *causes* are branded just like *products*. That means creating a compelling story around your cause is important in the same way Nike, Apple, or Starbucks creates a compelling story around their products. Sending a check is one thing, but *becoming identified with a great cause* takes it to a new level.

At the highest level, *being green* isn't just about helping the environment, it's about a *lifestyle that's changing the world*.

5) Mobile Technologies
I didn't fully realize the impact of mobile phone technology until I bought an iPhone. Up to that point, I had a fairly traditional cell phone that I used exclusively for – you won't believe

it – making phone calls. But when I started using an iPhone, I realized everything I had been missing – my complete (and multiple) address books, calendars, instant weather, maps, photos, email, text messaging, online videos, widgets and a host of other options that perform specific tasks from finding the nearest Mexican restaurant to movie times to package tracking and even daily Groucho Marx quotes.

The online encyclopedia Wikipedia reports that as of November 2007 the total number of mobile phone subscriptions worldwide reached 3.3 billion – or half of the human population – which makes the mobile phone the most widely used and most common gadget in the world.

Today, corporations – including TV networks and Hollywood movie studios – have jumped on the mobile phone bandwagon. In 2005, Walt Disney Studios partnered with Sprint to create a platform for their ESPN sports network. Since that time other companies like Verizon's "V Cast" have jumped into the fray with broadband programming designed to be viewed on mobile phones, generally up to five minutes long.

There are plenty of other entertainment competitors creating content for cell phones including Amp'd Mobile, MTV, Universal Studios, Apple, and Square Enix, Inc., a Japanese company, that produces game based-programs like "Final Fantasy" and "Dragon Quest." Companies like MobiTV, Cinema Electric, PocketCinema™ and plenty of others are upping the stakes as investors battle to reach this vast audience.

On the faith-based content side, companies like FaithFone Wireless™ and Faith Mobile are offering cell phone content such as daily devotionals, Bible passages, prayer of the day, life advice and like-minded entertainment content via (SMS) Text on branded mobile phone handsets.

Currently, the most popular entertainment-based uses of mobile phone technology are comedy, search and information.

In other words, few will be watching epics like "Star Wars" on a cell phone. More likely people will watch a short comedy sketch while waiting at the doctor's office, search for a local restaurant or access driving directions. I use multiple news widgets to scan for breaking news when I'm on the run and weather reports when I'm traveling.

Advertisers are currently excited over "opt-in" text messaging to consumers. While I can't imagine being interrupted throughout the day with advertisements on my mobile phone, millions of people are signing up. The important thing to realize is that these aren't blatant marketing campaigns. The advertisers are partnering with sports teams, news organizations and other outlets to deliver information people want – with a short end tag about a product or service.

For instance, you can sign up to receive updates on your favorite sports team or your flight, but at the end of the text, you'll see a plug for a related product. It's a strategy designed so it doesn't feel invasive to consumers because they are getting information they actually requested.

It's been proven that consumers are more willing to accept advertising messages for subjects or products they're interested in. So if someone fills out an information form at the mall about that hot new convertible on display, the car company knows the consumer will not be completely resistant to a text message with more information about that particular model, or news about special pricing. So, what does this mean for religious media programmers?

Relate your message to something that matters to people.

Keep it short. Find out the questions people are asking. For instance, I talked to a major movie studio executive the other day who enjoys a short, encouraging text message every morning from a popular media ministry. Others are doing devotions or tagging "opt-in" information with a promotional message about a Christian book or service.

Content providers for mobile phones are the real pioneers of the entertainment industry right now and they are operating with very few rules and a whole lot of unknowns. These companies are aggressive because they know that in the new media landscape success is often determined by who gets there first. For early adopters, brand recognition is critical. So being there first – even at great cost – can yield positive long-term brand identification.

Technologies like Twitter are changing the way people text message. You can now send multiple people a short "tweet" about what you're doing, where to meet – anything at all.

To many, a program like Twitter or a similar program called "Yammer" seems useless, and frankly, stupid. But Twitter has become so popular, so fast, that keeping up with its growing user base has become co-founders Jack Dorsey and Biz Stone's number one challenge. "Twitterers" (as they call themselves) post updates at Twitter.com or by using text or instant message tools – usually mobile phones or PDAs. It's a completely new communications paradigm as millions of young people engage in a steady stream of short messages (140 characters or less) about their lives. In fact, the impact of Twitter is so significant, people are already speculating that resumes of the future will be 140 characters or less.

And just to be clear, Twitter is not just about messages like "Meet me at the mall." I recently purchased a new software application for my iPhone and the company used Twitter posts to keep customers informed on a daily basis regarding bug fixes and upgrades.

Just imagine how you could use integrate Twitter, Yammer and similar programs into the life of your church or religious organization and be in constant communication with your audience?

THE TECHNOLOGY MIX

British telecom giant BT has encouraged employees to use a wide range of these new technologies and it's changing the way they do business. Some 10,500 BT employees are on Facebook, and more than 16,000 work in teams through online "wikis," which allow anyone to post notes, edit and make changes to project specifications, much like the online encyclopedia Wikipedia. With a global company like BT, every new project becomes a wiki, and teams around the world working from different time zones are able to edit, update and contribute anytime and anywhere – all online.

The company is also developing an internal social networking site which will allow leadership to spot people that form teams based on relationships and interests rather than mandates from above. With this new "organic" flow, a new class of communicators will emerge, and completely blow apart the traditional corporate organizational chart with its dotted lines and neat little boxes.

Could the organizational chart at your organization stand to be blown apart?

Some readers might consider applications like Facebook inappropriate for business. "Poking" people, requesting "friends" or writing on someone's "wall" just doesn't sound *serious*. What appears cute in high school or college, can appear quite silly in the boardroom; however, as a new generation enters the workforce, they will continue to adapt these platforms in new and ingenious ways. There is no question – it is and will continue to change the way we connect.

6) The Future of Blogging
Hi. My name is Phil and I'm a blogger. There, I said it.

Actually, I love writing my blog.

My friend and radio host Hugh Hewitt got me hooked, so from an addiction perspective, I don't know if I should consider him my blogging mentor or my drug dealer. My wife Kathleen considers blogging my mistress (although I don't think it's quite that bad).

For the uninitiated, blogging began as a simple online diary – a "weblog." That name was soon abbreviated into "blog," and today there are more than a hundred million blogs on the web. The web giant, Technorati.com tracks blogs and lists them by topic, popularity, and links among others.

I started my blog at philcooke.com to write about issues like faith and media, and I normally write at least one post per day. Other blogs have multiple contributors, but I write mine solo, and as I told my assistant recently, after dealing with business all day, it saves me a great deal of money on therapy.

A SIMPLE BLOG CAN HAVE A WORLDWIDE AUDIENCE

Blogging allows me to vent and to create a conversation about issues in the religious media world that doesn't exist anywhere else. As a result, I have contributors that respond to my posts from the United States, Canada, Australia, Africa and all across Europe.

During the controversy surrounding the movie, "The Da Vinci Code," I wrote a post on how the Christian community should engage in a dialogue about the film. Little did I know that at the same time the political and religious leaders of the Philippines were debating about whether or not to ban the film in their country. I discovered a few weeks later that the editor of the daily newspaper in Manila, Philippines read my blog, pulled my post, and re-printed it on the front page of the paper as an example of how the country should deal with the movie.

It only takes about 15 minutes to set up a blogging account with free software available on the web. It's something literally anyone can do; especially if you have something to say – and often.

People ask me where I find ideas to write about or how I process enough information and news for the material on my blog. It's a great question, because if we're going to engage the culture, whether you write a blog or not, it's critical to be aware of the issues we are facing. As such, developing a system for digesting information, and then thinking about it and processing it will make a dramatic difference in your ideas, your strategies and your intellectual depth. My method is nothing stupendous, but here's what works for me:

1. I wake up every morning around 6:30 a.m. and work out at least 3-4 days a week. While working out, I alternate between viewing CNN, traditional networks and Fox News. It's always interesting to note the different perspectives on each of the networks. I also watch a few music videos on MTV or VH1 to keep up on what's happening in that world and even scan some religious media programming on the religious networks.

2. During breakfast, I read the *Los Angeles Times* for the liberal side of things and the *Wall Street Journal* for the conservative side. I also look through the *Los Angeles Daily News* for a more middle of the road perspective. If I'm traveling I read the local paper in whatever city I'm working.

3. From a weekly newsmagazine perspective, I subscribe to *Time* and *World*. Honestly, I have a magazine fetish, so I also get sports, religion, technology and cultural magazines including *Christianity Today*, *Fast Company*, and *Image Journal*.

4. While there are many great RSS platforms to choose from, my personal favorite RSS reader is Yahoo. It's based on RSS widgets that allow you to fill a single page with multiple RSS feeds from different sources and customize their size and placement. Rather than a single page for one RSS, having many different RSS feeds allows you to scan them easily. In addition, the site

allows you to have multiple pages, with each page designed according to preference. So in my case, I have:

- A Branding page of RSS feeds from my favorite sources on branding and marketing (7 feeds)
- A Media page of RSS feeds from various media sources (6 feeds)
- A News page from news sources (6 feeds)
- A Religious page with multiple sources (6 feeds)
- A Weather page (Although I actually prefer the weather widget on my iPhone)
- An Entertainment page featuring YouTube, AOL Video and various other online entertainment sources

The best thing about Yahoo is that it allows you total control of the size and placement of the feeds. So I can easily get 6-7 feeds on a single page, which keeps me from scrolling through long lists of information.

Here's the point – you want information about what's happening in the world, but you need to be able to go through it efficiently. You defeat the purpose of being engaged in the world around you if all you do is sit around all day watching the news and reading magazines.

That's why I incorporate information gathering into part of my daily routine:

- Get the morning TV news while working out.
- Read the papers during breakfast.
- Catch up on my magazines or write during plane trips (being trapped on a plane makes you wonderfully productive).
- Scan through RSS feeds first thing after arriving in the office.

By the time you start working each day, you're ready to use that information to beat the competition, create new projects and do your work more effectively. My system may not work for you, but the important thing is to develop something – your own system – so you can get the information you need to make a difference in the world around you.

And don't get discouraged! We live in an age of information overload. The Daniel Yankelovich Group estimates that an average citizen in an urban area may be confronted with up to 5,000 advertising messages per day. That's up from about 2,000 messages in the 1970s.

DON'T JUST SEEK MORE INFORMATION, SEEK WISDOM

In the digital age, our challenge is not the pursuit of *information*, but rather the pursuit of *discernment*. It's not about *search* – it's about *filters*. Having the right filters (in this case RSS feeds) can be crucial in helping you access the right information at the right time.

And just to deflect any critical mail, I should add, when it comes to serious reading, I never multitask. News, blogs and informational updates can be crammed into multiple places in various ways, but serious reading takes time, focus and concentration.

In a world where information overload is so promient, take the time for serious reading and reflection. The kind of reading you can only find in serious novels and non-fiction books are critical for a deeper level of development. News can provide *information*, but a great leader needs *insight*. The decisions you make based on the available information need to be tempered with a deeper understanding of human relationships, the arts, psychology, history, culture, politics, theology and doctrine.

There are a lot of diseases I deal with on a daily basis that have infected the church, but one of the most serious is shallow thinking.

When pastors and Christian leaders don't have a deep intellectual bench, the solutions they offer end up being shallow, simplistic and weak.

Intellectually, too many pastors are creampuffs.

If we're going to engage the culture in a significant way, we need to raise up more intellectuals within the church; men and women who have wrestled with the big questions and have a deep understanding of the challenges facing the next generation.

CHAPTER ELEVEN
A LOOK AT THE FUTURE OF CHRISTIAN MEDIA

THE BEST WAY TO PREDICT THE FUTURE IS TO INVENT IT.
– ALAN KAY, APPLE COMPUTER

THE FUTURE IS NOT SOME PLACE WE ARE GOING TO, BUT ONE WE ARE CREATING. THE PATHS ARE NOT TO BE FOUND, BUT MADE, AND THE ACTIVITY OF MAKING THEM, CHANGES BOTH THE MAKER AND THE DESTINATION.
– JOHN SCHAAR, FUTURIST

I'm sure sometime in the future I'll regret this chapter because the entire media business is an industry that's volatile and in the grip of powerful change. Hopefully, 10 years from now you won't be writing a book about my mistakes. I'm certainly not a prophet (and thankful I can't be stoned if I'm wrong), but I'm on the inside of the industry, so perhaps my model should be more like John the Baptist crying in the wilderness.

With that in mind, allow me to change into my camel hair suit and grab a bite of locust and wild honey and then take a shot about what we can expect to happen with religious media in the future.

First, let's change the name.
It won't be the "Christian media" anymore. Instead, it will be "Christians who create media." In the next few years, my dream is that we climb out of the ghetto and pop the bubble. The next generation couldn't care less about creating a safe media harbor where they can be protected from the world. Twenty years ago

young Christian college students studied media to work at a Christian TV or radio network. But today, Christian students want to go to Hollywood and impact the industry; a great many media directors and staff working at local churches dream of someday creating a mainstream movie or TV series.

As I've said before, I don't have a problem with creating explicitly Christian programming designed for Christian audiences. There's a place for programs about Christian teaching, theology and family life, but let's stop making it so corny and cheesy. Let's start making content that is accessible to everyone. The early church would have never considered a service without the involvement of non-believers. Those early followers of Jesus spoke the language of the culture and engaged the outside world on a daily basis.

This is my plea: whatever you produce – movies, TV, digital media, web-based content, mobile entertainment, whatever – produce to *include*, not *exclude*. At Cooke Pictures, our goal is to create programming that any audience will respect. Even if they don't agree with our theology or central theme, at least they'll walk away acknowledging it was a powerful and compelling program or movie.

And if that happens, we've at least opened the door.

Drop the lingo, toss out the clichés and become more comfortable speaking the language of the culture. You don't have to use the same metaphors Jesus used. After all, how many people today know much about planting seeds, raising cattle, or putting old wine into new wineskins? The truths are in the principles not necessarily the illustrations. Outside of reciting the actual scriptures, Jesus didn't use the same metaphors as Moses. He understood that culture changes and he needed to speak to people in the language of His time. I'm reminded of a missionary who struggled sharing the biblical concept of the "bread of life" with his congregation on a

Pacific Island. After much frustration, he tried the "banana of life" and suddenly their faces lit up. The meaning finally came alive.

What is the language of your time? How can you adapt the message of Jesus into the language and metaphors of today?

Second, embrace secular media.

Few people in your office will know anything about the TV evangelist you listened to last night, but they will all know what happened on *American Idol*. Start watching and using media as a bridge to connect to people in your community. The movie theater is "church" for this generation of young people – it's where they learn behavior, morals and ideals. If you're not familiar with those stories you can't have a voice in those conversations. Understand the influence the media has with this generation and be prepared to use it as a pathway to relationship.

And stop hindering young people from pursuing careers in Hollywood! If we want to impact the culture, we need Christians in Hollywood more than anywhere else. I was interviewed on a radio program recently and a few days later I received a letter from a mother who said:

Dear Mr. Cooke:
My son is 16-years-old, and all his life he's wanted to be involved in the movie business. But as a Christian, I've always been afraid of the entertainment industry and time and time again tried to stop his dream. He begged to attend film school, but I told him I wouldn't help. I tried to stop him from attending movies, because I knew that would only feed his passion. I wasn't trying to be a bad mother. I was just terrified of what might happen to him should he go into that industry.

But after listening to you on the radio, I realized that I was wrong. I've spent his whole life trying to stop him from what he believes God is calling him to do. Because of my fear, I was keeping him from achieving his dream. Since your interview, we've discussed his future, and started looking for a film school, and I'm fully prepared to support him as he begins this journey. Thank you for helping me realize that God speaks in a variety of ways, and how important it is to communicate with this generation in a way they understand.

My heart broke thinking about all the years this mother had fought her own son out of fear and ignorance. Chances are, she would have been perfectly happy had he wanted to be a producer for a local *Christian* program, but God was calling him to a different path.

This isn't to say that professionals in the religious media community are somehow less important than those in the secular media community. Listen to your heart – don't be afraid to embrace your call in either direction.

Certainly, there is gratuitous violence, sexuality and profanity on network television, in the movies and easily accessible online. Although it is important to be cautious and keep a watchful eye, remember that after the resurrection of Christ, 11 people changed the world because they weren't afraid of risk. Encourage young people in your church to pursue a career in entertainment or media. Start a movie club as a small group and discuss popular culture and how we can engage the community. Running back to the bubble out of fear does nothing for the cause of Christ in the culture.

THE PAULIST MODEL

One of my early inspirations for working outside the bubble was Father Ellwood "Bud" Kieser, a Catholic priest who founded Paulist Productions (paulistproductions.org) in 1960. During the 1960s, Kieser produced a series called "Insight," a weekly dramatic program consisting of thirty minute comedies or dramas focused on social or religious themes and featuring major stars of the time. The highly acclaimed series shed light on the human condition through creative and poignant stories and won five Emmy Awards during its 23-year run.

Paulist Productions went on to produce feature films like "Romero" in 1989 and "Entertaining Angels: The Dorothy Day Story" in 1996 – both released by Warner Brothers. Father Frank Desiderio is the current president of the company and has expanded it's programming to include cable documentaries and now an online digital video series called "Tyler's Ride." The organization is also associated with The Humanitas Prize, which is awarded to film and television writers whose work not only entertains, but also enriches the viewing public.

Paulist Productions has never lived in the religious media bubble, and since it's inception has competed with major Hollywood production companies for access to mainstream TV networks and movie theaters. As a result, their work is hardly known inside religious media circles, but it's making a significant impact in the greater culture.

Third, the media will become a mash-up.
At it's most basic level, "mash-ups" are web applications that allow you to mix and match different elements for different applications. Examples would be adding a time-zone clock to a travel document, mixing a mapping program with a real estate site or data mash-ups that combine research information with similar practical applications.

From a media perspective, in the future, people will use a wide range of media for vastly different purposes – mixing and matching at will. In this context, I use the term "mash-ups" to also include *personal media discrimination*. I'm referring to consumers who use a wide variety of media – sometimes adapting it in new and innovative ways.

My iPhone combines a cell phone, navigation, email, text messaging, entertainment options and more. I still want my big screen TV for the Super Bowl, but it also connects to my laptop so I can access ESPN's game time analysis. I keep my iPod in my briefcase so I can listen to music or watch a movie while traveling but since my iPhone also is a music and video player, the lines are quickly bluring.

Consumers are moving toward integrated applications that allow them a wider range of control.

Remember my earlier comments about the millennial generation wanting to be part of a dialogue; they want their voice to be heard, but the also want a choice about their media options and how their technology works together. What's more – they don't care how the content gets there or what type of channel it's on.

> **MY KIDS DON'T KNOW THE DIFFERENCE BETWEEN CABLE AND BROADCAST. BROADBAND DELIVERY IS JUST ANOTHER WAY OF DELIVERING IT TO THE HOME. TIVO'S VIEW IS [TO] MAKE IT TOTALLY IRRELEVANT TO THE CONSUMER WHETHER THEY'RE USING THAT REMOTE TO GET A BROADCAST CHANNEL, A CABLE CHANNEL, OR BROADBAND CONTENT.**
> – TOM ROGERS, PRESIDENT OF TIVO

What does this mean for producers of faith-based content? It means two things:

1) A TV or radio program isn't enough anymore.

2) People don't care where their favorite content comes from.

But religious producers still don't understand how the media mix works together to impact consumers.

Just yesterday I received a call from a video producer for one of the largest church denominations in America about their new commercial for national television. It wasn't a bad spot, but when I asked him about the overall media strategy for the campaign, he fell silent.

When I asked why, he replied with a response I've heard many times before: "We had a production deadline and that deadline drove the project. Plus, the producer knew a guy at a famous animation studio for the effects and a popular Christian recording artist donated the song so we went ahead and did the spot."

The producers only did part of the work, and that part they did backwards.

NEVER START WITH A DEADLINE

I've discovered when deadlines drive projects, the really important things like "values" and "creativity" are often forgotten or overlooked. Second, don't do it because a friend knows someone or a celebrity donates a song. Third, what about all the other connections to the message? The website, the response mechanism and other messaging tools?

Because the team at that major denomination doesn't understand the strategic role of mixing media, that TV spot (a very expensive one!) will never make an impact.

Media strategy means more than just creating an effective radio or TV commercial. It means indentifying the audience you want to reach, understanding how they want to connect, providing a website or other means for that connection to take place, planning a response vehicle and providing for follow up. In the media mix of the future, a web presence will often be the hub of a campaign. Using websites, blogs, mobile media, or social networking applications, the "connection" will be the central thread that coordinates entire campaigns.

Could we create a sister campaign for mobile phones? What about a corresponding radio spot (or series of spots)? What about a short, branded entertainment piece? There are lots of elements in the media mix that must be considered. If you're only doing radio or TV or a website, then you're missing huge opportunities to reach and communicate with your audience.

GONE ARE THE DAYS OF 'ONE SHOW, ONE ADVERTISING CAMPAIGN.' NOW YOU'VE GOT TO ENGAGE CUSTOMERS ON EVERY LEVEL.

– TREVOR EDWARDS, VICE PRESIDENT OF GLOBAL BRAND
AND CATEGORY MANAGEMENT, NIKE

The future of your message depends upon your ability to utilize digital components. A digital plan should be a fundamental part of your overall strategy, not some type of add-on or afterthought. Mark Parker, Nike's CEO has said, "The Nike brand will always be our strongest asset, but consumers are looking for new relevance and connections."

One of the key characteristics of the millennial generation is that they effortlessly move across multiple platforms. For baby boomers, a movie trailer was enough to lure us to the theater for a new movie. Today, trailers are only the beginning. Behind the scenes interviews on network TV, lost scenes, text messages, trivia contests, full-featured websites, tie-ins to network news and online communities are the basis of a complete promotional campaign.

Granted, if you're a leader, and not involved full-time in the world of digital media, keeping up with the options and changes can be a real challenge. Just when you thought you'd mastered names like Napster, Facebook, Myspace, Flickr and YouTube, you're confronted with new names like Picasa, Photobucket, BitTorrent, Vimeo, and Skype, entering the lexicon.

By the time you read this, there will be many more options on the market that don't even exist today.

THIS IS THE FIRST TIME THAT PROGRAMMING WITH THE DISTRIBUTION POTENTIAL OF NBC UNIVERSAL WILL BE CENTERED FROM THE START AROUND ADVERTISERS.

– MATT SPIEGEL, CEO, OMG DIGITAL

The walls between advertising and programming are dissolving. "Branded content" is the term used for programming that is really focused around a commercial brand. A few years ago, I directed a 15 minute dramatic short film for a beverage company in Japan. It was designed to play on the company's website and it eventually toured the film festival circuit. At the time, the company didn't even show the product in the film – they simply wanted a heroic story associated with the brand.

Today, branded content ranges from programming featuring a specific product to shows where the product is hardly, if ever, mentioned. However, it is the *connection* to the product or lifestyle that is critical.

The most popular example of branded content is a recent segment of an episodic drama where the producers wrote an entire scene around a new razor blade. A recent movie was completely funded because the entire story took place inside a big-box electronics store. I have a friend in this business, and he attends film festivals offering producers significant funding for their projects if they'll just integrate one or more of his client's products into their story.

In a world where 30-second spots no longer rule, advertisers are looking for new ways to make an impression on viewers. But there's a risky balance involved. As Bob Bernstein, chief media officer at Draftfcb recently said, "It takes a very delicate balance. Producers and marketers need to make sure their products and services are part of the story and not a disruption to it."

Fourth, pastors will be a new center of innovation.
The first generation of Christian TV leaders were most often evangelists, working outside a particular church affiliation. Men like Billy Graham, Oral Roberts, Pat Robertson, Paul Crouch, Jim Bakker, Morris Cerullo, or Lester Sumrall. Certainly there were a few pastors like Rex Humbard, Robert Schuller, and later Fred Price, Rod Parsley or Creflo Dollar, but individual

churches didn't play a significant role in the early development of Christian television. Radio was similar, as early broadcasters hailed from a variety of backgrounds and affiliations.

Today, most of the innovation is coming from local pastors using the media. Pastor Joel Osteen produces the most successful inspirational program on television from Lakewood Church in Houston. T.D. Jakes is creating a television, movie and print empire from The Potter's House in Dallas. Ed Young at Fellowship Church in Dallas is training pastors to be more creative. These and many others are *leading the charge toward change* as the next generation of media leaders.

The style and approach of these pastors is far wider than the first generation of broadcasters. As I mentioned before, Pastors Erwin McManus in Los Angeles and Rob Bell in Grand Rapids are producing short films. Mark Crow in Oklahoma City has created a IPTV network, Mark Gungor in Green Bay is focusing on marriage programming, Gary Keesee in Columbus is using television to help people with their finances, Bil Cornelius in Corpus Christi is empowering the local business community, Jack Graham in Dallas is strategically using radio and television together, Greg Groeschel in Oklahoma City is exploring what the online church could be, and the list goes on. In addition, hundreds of these pastors are blogging on a variety of issues and themes.

Why pastors? I think there are many reasons. Pastors have an initial financial base with a local congregation that can help fund the start-up costs of media. Tax laws may also help a local church more than a typical non-profit ministry. Plus, creating programming every week through worship services is a convenient way to launch into the content necessary to sustain a media ministry.

Local churches also have physical facilities already in place, as well as access to a younger generation of media savvy members, ready to jump at the chance to create innovative content for short films, commercials, websites and digital media.

At the national level, I'm noticing a second generation of pastors that are uniquely different from their famous fathers. Although the first generation leaders launched influential media ministries and certainly left their mark, second generation leaders like Joel Osteen, Jonathan Falwell and Ed Young are pioneering their own unique paths and developing their own voices – often dramatically different from those of their fathers.

Fifth, it will be producer-driven instead of preacher-driven.
These and other pastors and ministry leaders are indeed helping change the paradigm in religious media. However, there's a deeper change coming, and that's the move from "preacher driven" to "producer driven" programming.

While there will always be a place in the media for important and timely preaching, that source of programming will not be the driver of Christian media in the future. As I've already pointed out, there are young and creative independent producers creating low budget movies, short films, Internet radio programming, innovative websites and podcasts – we must find them and encourage what they're doing.

This is not meant to discourage pastors or ministry leaders from creating compelling programming based on teaching and preaching. Many of our clients at Cooke Pictures are preaching ministries, and we've helped them create brand identities that capture significant audiences. But at the same time, we must also look for a wider range of programming options and build up the creative men and women who can make new programming a reality.

The first generation of religious media communicators were, for the most part pastors and evangelists, who seized upon radio and eventually television as a way to extend their reach. Their strength was the power of their message. They preached with passion and excitement, and were relentless in their mission to spread the gospel.

But their weakness was packaging – the various elements such as lighting, set design, wardrobe, directing, and editing that make up a quality program. They were preachers after all, and had little expertise about production techniques, contemporary graphics, branding or compelling visuals. The resulting programs, although they shared an important message, were often corny, low quality, and poorly produced. To non-believers, they appeared fake, cheesy, and insincere.

Today, the driving force behind Christian media is emerging from behind the camera.

In the secular advertising world, and in response to the digital media shift, I'm seeing the growth of a new type of marketing expert. Some call the position a "Super Chief Marketing Officer." The role would be played by someone not only versed in *traditional* media and advertising, but whose expertise and passion also encompasses the *open world of digital media.* It's much the same with television networks. They're looking for producers and programmers that understand how to take a TV concept from the traditional media schedule and make it work in the digital frontier.

Who's that person in your organization? Who is your "super" producer or programmer, who understands both traditional and digital media? If you don't have that person on staff, then it's time to partner with a consultant, agency or outside producer who can bring that perspective to your ministry.

Younger filmmakers and producers want to expand the horizons of religious media, try new techniques and create projects for wide ranging audiences. These producers are looking beyond telethons to fund their projects and are experimenting with commercial sponsorship, grants and product placement.

As a result, some preachers are catching the vision. Just because you preach, doesn't mean the program has to be old fashioned, and through innovative production techniques, a younger generation of pastors and ministry leaders are discovering how to reach an audience and motivate them to respond.

Sixth, future content creators will understand the impact of culture. It's been a long and difficult road, but a wide range of Christian writers, speakers, artists and media professionals have made a compelling case for the importance of understanding the impact of culture – and the Christian community is finally listening. A generation of pastors (my father for instance) attended seminaries to be trained in theology and doctrine, but graduated with little knowledge of the surrounding culture in which they would be ministering.

It is inconceivable to think we would send missionaries out into the field without arming them with significant knowledge of the language, customs, traditions and culture in which they would be serving; and yet understanding our own culture was rarely a priority for pastoral training here at home. Today seminaries are finally beginning to understand the importance of understanding our culture.

For instance, Fuller Seminary in Pasadena, California recently opened the Brehm Center, an innovative space for the creative integration of worship, theology and arts in culture. Writers and thinkers such as Craig Detweiler, author of *A Matrix of Meanings: Finding God in Popular Culture*, Dick Staub, author of *The Culturally Savvy Christian*, Andy Crouch, author of *Culture Making: Recovering our Creative Calling*, and Robert Johnston, author of *Reel Spirituality: Theology and Film in Dialogue*, are training a new generation of ministry leaders to work more effectively within the surrounding culture.

Many – particularly in Hollywood – attribute the late Bob Briner's stirring book, *Roaring Lambs: A Gentle Plan to Radically*

Change Your World, as instrumental in igniting their passion to
engage and impact the culture.

**Seventh, the open media environment will change everything
you know about church – and more.**
The digital media revolution is far more than the rise of social networks or the ability to watch comedy clips on your cell
phone. Our future is "open" media – which will have massive
implications for culture, politics, education, business and religion. It will cause a massive shift in the way we find, process
and relate to information – and it's impact will spill over into
relationships, faith and family structures.

Christopher Vollmer captured the concept well in his
book, *Always On: Advertising, Marketing, and Media in an Era
of Consumer Control*. He uses the term "always on" because
they consumer is always present, constantly being bombarded
with a constant stream of media messages.

Take a notebook and just list all the intersections you have
with media today – not just your TV, radio, computer, iPod, or
mobile phone – but with billboards, print ads, commercials on
monitors at the gas pump, video monitors in elevators, background audio at the mall, movie trailers and digital signage to
name a few.

The *New York Times* reported about this phenomenon: that
supermarket eggs have been stamped with the names of CBS
TV shows, US Airways has placed ads on motion sickness bags
and subway turnstiles display Geico auto insurance advertising. As I write this, the Federal Government Security Agency
TSA has "sold" the plastic bins that run through airport security
lines to advertisers, so millions of travelers will now be hit with
advertising messages every time they go through security.

*In an world that is always "on," we can't escape the influence of
the media.*

However, the open media world has moved beyond the antiquated concept of simply *viewing* advertising. Vollmer describes a primary lesson of the new media world: "It doesn't matter how many people are watching; what counts is whether they're paying attention and responding."

Let me explain the change in this way:

In the world of closed, traditional media:
- Political power was the method of choice for impacting culture
- Famous pastors and evangelists were celebrities
- Christian leaders could control information
- Every programmer wanted to be on TBN or Salem Broadcasting
- TV was the hub of marketing, advertising, and entertainment
- Programmers controlled the message
- Consumers bought what marketers and advertisers promoted
- YouTube and Facebook were simply fads
- Mobile phones were for making calls
- Bloggers were a little nutty
- A church controlled it's membership
- A ministry or non-profit decided how to talk to its donors
- The audience watched or listened to what you wanted them to see or hear

But in the open media revolution:
- Cultural engagement is the way to impact the world
- Personality driven ministry is on the decline
- Information can't be controlled
- Traditional networks will exist, but they aren't the nexus of power and influence they once were – nor are they the only key to reaching your audience.
- TV has become TIVO
- The audience influences the message
- Consumers buy what their friends endorse
- YouTube content is as good as traditional advertising
- Mobile phones will become the single most important gadget in people's lives

- Bloggers are the new influencers and authorities. They even cost a national network news anchor his job
- "Church membership" will experience a radical re-think
- Donors decide how to talk to organizations
- The audience is in charge

From a communication perspective our world has transformed from a one-way model to a two-way, dynamic conversation.

I've already discussed how the next generation wants to have a voice, and this desire is impacting everything – from media and education to business and politics and even worship.

> CONSUMERS ARE TELLING US THAT THEY WANT TO BE IN CONTROL OF THE STORYTELLING. AND, AS A PART OF THAT DESIRE, THEY WANT TO ENGAGE IN ADVERTISING IN DIFFERENT WAYS. THERE WILL BE TIMES WHEN THE OLD KIND OF PASSIVE EXPERIENCE IS GOING TO BE JUST RIGHT. BUT INCREASINGLY, CONSUMERS WANT TO FILTER, THEY WANT TO ACT, THEY WANT TO BE PART OF THE EX-PERIENCE. AND WE HAVE TO BE SMART ABOUT IT.
> – BETH COMSTOCK, PRESIDENT OF INTEGRATED MEDIA, NBC/UNIVERSAL

Many traditional pastors and Christian leaders will recoil at this concept because they're used to running the show. After all (and I say this with respect), pastors are today's "paid professionals of religion" and they're supposed to be the man or woman in charge.

That thinking reminds me of William Tyndale and his struggle to translate the Bible into English during the 16th century. At the time, church authorities were determined to keep control of the populace, and the best way to do that was to have exclusive power over Biblical interpretation.

When Tyndale began translating the Bible, the church was all about control, and they were deadly serious. It was illegal to be in possession of an English Bible because church leaders weren't interested in individual interpretation. One young man was burned at the stake for having a fragment of the 23rd Psalm in his pocket written in English.

Tyndale fled England, lived among smugglers, spent his adult life under an alias and had his printing presses destroyed multiple times but never gave up. As he translated, pages of his work were smuggled into England inside bales of hay, clothing and barrels of food. Friends inside England would take the pages and have them bound and distributed inside the country.

Years after Tyndale's eventual capture and execution, when the King finally authorized an English translation (which appeared in 1611), it's been said that people filled St. Paul's Cathedral in London just to listen to the Bible being read in their own language. They would sit for hours as one person would stand at the pulpit reading. When that person would grow tired, another one would stand up and continue. People were transfixed as they heard God's Word for the first time in their own language. I often remember that story when I think of the digital revolution that's happening today.

As the next generation searches for meaning, are we going to continue trying to control the message, or are we going to be more open – allowing the people a voice in how they communicate, relate, and respond?

In the digital-driven world, here are some questions you need to be asking:

1) How much do I know about how my congregation, donors, partners or audience interact with our organization?
Who likes what? How well are you segmented? This isn't about computerized mailing lists that simply categorize people. It's

about having a more intimate relationship with your audience so you know how they prefer to communicate. Knowing the people you're talking to, and then listening to their response, matters in the digital media world.

2) Does your media mix reflect that audience?
Have you based your media strategy (radio, TV, web, IPTV, etc) on your target audience? Are you reaching them in the way they want to be reached? Are you maximizing the media tools at your disposal to help tell your story?

3) How do influencers view your ministry or organization?
In a networked world, the impact of other leaders "talking you up" can be significant. Networks matter because people are so-cial beings. What have you done to foster relationships with other like-minded churches, organizations or leaders? When-ever other bloggers discuss the things I've written at philcooke. com, it drives up my traffic. What are you doing to get people talking?

4) Are you considered a truth-teller?
Is your ministry reliable? Does it provide real answers to the questions your congregation is wrestling with? In other words, are you answering the questions people are asking? Are your answers honest and authentic? Pastor Tim Keller of Redeemer Presbyterian Church in New York City says it this way, "You have to adapt to people's questions."

5) Have you changed the culture at your organization to re-flect the new paradigm?
Are you embracing teams and allowing for competing voices in your organization? Are you more interested in squeezing the most out of people or inspiring them to accomplish great things? Are you allowing online connectivity to motivate and self-organize your employees?

6) Are you marketing or influencing?

Are you allowing your audience to influence your message? Or are you still delivering that message as a monologue?

7) Are you acting on the feedback you're hearing from your audience?

Are you dictating to your audience or responding to their feedback?

As I write this manuscript, Senator Barack Obama was just elected our next president, defeating the Republican candidate, Senator John McCain. Leading up to the election, *Wall Street Journal* columnist Peggy Noonan wrote about the differences between the two candidates. As I read her analysis, I realized she was capturing a bigger picture – the comparison between the closed world of the past, and the open world of the future. Regardless of what you think of the candidates' political positions, Noonan's analysis is a fascinating look at the difference between the two cultures:

> In the Old America, love of country was natural. You breathed it in. You either loved it or knew you should.
>
> In the New America, love of country is a decision. It's one you make after weighing the pros and cons. What you breathe in is skepticism and a heightened appreciation of the global view.
>
> Old America: Tradition is a guide in human affairs.
> New America: Tradition is a challenge, a barrier, or a lovely antique.
>
> The Old America had big families. You married and had children. Life happened to you. You didn't decide, it decided. Now it's all on you.
>
> Old America, when life didn't work out: "Luck of the draw!"
> New America when life doesn't work: "I made bad choices!"

Old America: "I had faith, and trust."
New America: "You had limited autonomy!"

Old America: "We've been here three generations."
New America: "You're still here?"

Old America: We have to have a government, but that doesn't mean I have to love it.
New America: We have to have a government and I am desperate to love it.

Old America: Politics is a duty.
New America: Politics is life.

The Old America: Religion is good.
The New America: Religion is problematic.

The Old: Smoke 'em if you got 'em.
The New: I'll sue.

Mr. McCain is the old world of concepts like "personal honor," of a manliness that was a style of being, of an attachment to the fact of higher principles.

Mr. Obama is the new world, which is marked in part by doubt as to the excellence of the old. It prizes ambivalence as proof of thoughtfulness, as evidence of a textured seriousness.

This quote isn't meant to be a commentary on political candidates, but a glimpse at the competing ways each generation views the world. The point isn't *agreement*, it's *enlightenment*. We're never going to communicate effectively if we don't understand how differing audiences view the world.

Generation after generation of pastors and Christian leaders have gotten it wrong by believing our only responsibility, as Christians, is to share the message – but we also have a responsibility to make sure our message is effectively communicated.

To be honest, this new digital two-way conversation is remarkably similar to the method of worship during the days of the early church. Frank Viola and George Barna, writing in their book, *Pagan Christianity: Exploring The Roots Of Our Church Practices*, reveal some of the most common practices of worship in the early church including:

- Active participation and interruptions by the audience were common.
- Prophets and priests spoke extemporaneously and out of a present burden, rather than from a set script.
- There is no indication that Old Testament prophets or priests gave regular speeches to God's people. Instead, the nature of Old Testament preaching was sporadic, fluid, and open for audience participation. Preaching in the ancient synagogue followed a similar pattern.

Wayne E. Oates, writing in *Protestant Pastoral Counseling*, put it this way:

> The original proclamation of the Christian message was a two-way conversation... but when the oratorical schools of the Western world laid hold of the Christian message, they made Christian preaching something vastly different. Oratory tended to take the place of conversation. The greatness of the orator took the place of the astounding event of Jesus Christ. And the dialogue between speaker and listener faded into a monologue.

That's not to say that preaching or proclaiming the gospel isn't important, but it does indicate how new technology is actually giving us the capability to recover many of the styles and ideals of the early church. The two-way conversation that began in Jerusalem became a one-way conversation under the influence of Greco-Roman culture; and now in the digital age, we are once-again rediscovering the power of dialogue over monologue.

Simply put, in the open world of the future, those who simply preach or teach without regard to the way the audience understands and responds will be left behind.

Eighth, the mass media is dying.

The concept of connecting people will take on a whole new meaning in the open world. Television was once called a vast wasteland, and it's hard to argue with that description. Even today, with multiple cable and satellite channels, religious and family channels, and other positive signs, there are still a lot of desert out there in the media landscape.

> **THE WEB AS INTERACTION BETWEEN PEOPLE IS REALLY WHAT THE WEB IS. THAT WAS WHAT IT WAS DESIGNED TO BE, A COLLABORATIVE SPACE WHERE PEOPLE CAN INTERACT.**
> – TIM BERNERS-LEE, CO-FOUNDER, WORLD WIDE WEB

Today – media is about personalization. The "mass audience" isn't interested in the same thing anymore, they tasted customization and there is no going back. On my digital music player, I have classic rock and roll, bluegrass, praise and worship, Frank Sinatra, Broadway, southern gospel and even opera. I'm not interested in what radio stations *think* I need – now I can customize my own playlist.

So what does this mean for those of us interested in sharing our faith or selling products through the media? It means it's time to wake up to the change.

In the church, pastors, Christian leaders and broadcasters always thought we knew what our audience wanted, and more importantly, that they would listen to our message. But today, as I've said before, the audience is in charge. In a virtually unlimited channel universe, the audience has more choices than ever, and for us to justify their attention, we need to get on their wavelength.

Stop thinking "mass" and start thinking "niche." Small is the new big.

It's important to find the story that surrounds your life and ministry. What do people think of when they think of you? If you can pinpoint your own brand story – why you do what you do, who you really are, what your gifts and talents are, and what makes you different – then you can start to find the potential audience that would connect with your message.

The Bible tells us that people walked away from Jesus. Some felt his message was too harsh, others felt it required too great a change, and more than a few probably thought he was crazy. There were towns where the unbelief was so great, it was impossible to break through.

IF JESUS COULDN'T REACH EVERYBODY, NEITHER CAN YOU

I grow weary of the small churches of 25 people meeting in a rented office who call themselves a "World Outreach Center." I appreciate the vision, but let's think a bit more realistically.

Ask most pastors about their mission statement, and they'll tell you *"To reach the nations with the gospel."* But is that really possible? Is it realistic?

In the digital media era of the future, scaling down actually helps you grow. It's not about reaching the "nations," it's about reaching your "niche." The question you should be asking is: *What do your specific gifts, your passion, and your brand story say about your potential audience?*

When it comes to "reaching the nations" if we'd all give up on that noble sounding goal, and focus on the specific audience we are called to reach, then together, we could actually reach the world.

For instance, one pastor with the noble but vague vision of "reaching the world" hit a plateau. He tried everything but just couldn't push his attendance past a few hundred. But when he really considered his passion and gifting, he realized that he felt most called to reach *men*. After all, most men find church an excruciating experience, and not nearly enough feel comfortable inside the doors of a typical church building.

So the pastor narrowed his focus to reach a *smaller* audience (men), and to his surprise, his church started growing. Today it's more than tripled in size and still growing. He discovered that by focusing on a more targeted audience, your potential for growth is far greater.

WHAT ABOUT CHRISTIAN MUSIC?

In the July / August 2008 issue of *Collide Magazine*, Scott McClellan wrote a feature story based on music producer Charlie Peacock's assessment that the Christian music industry is dying. According to Peacock, the five most important issues are:

1) The major labels aren't in danger of going under anytime soon, but they'll be forced to depend on dwindling revenue from their song catalogs.

2) The term CCM, or *Christian Contemporary Music*, will go away.

3) Christian music that matters won't have any affiliation with the Christian music industry but instead will be written, recorded, and released in the mainstream.

4) Worship music serves a purpose within the church, which guarantees its survival.

5) The big names from CCM's glory days (Michael W. Smith, Amy Grant, Steven Curtis Chapman, etc.) will survive, but

many artists from the last decade will be left looking for a reason, roaming through the night to find their place in the world.

While, as McClellan states, the charges aren't exactly blasphemy, they did set off quite the controversy within the industry.

David Sessions, editor of *Patrol*, an online music and media magazine (patrolmag.com) agreed: "The best thing that can happen is for people to forget entirely that they once specified whether their music was 'Christian' or 'mainstream.' That divide has been the single most damaging idea to Christianity in the modern world."

Peacock echoed that indictment: "Anyone who has studied CCM knows that it's front-loaded with a very specious strategy - that is, the creation of a youth-oriented music to counteract the undesirable youth-oriented music of the culture at large. [That strategy] probably looked righteous in the beginning but proved very flawed."

McClellan covers both sides of the issue, but the article does point to a deep divide in the world of Christian music. Should it continue to exist as a niche industry? Should Christians move more into mainstream music? Can the business model hold up – should it?

In a feature story in *Christianity Today* magazine on the issue, music marketing consultant Mark Joseph points out:

>...the real question is, why should bands have to follow such a circuitous path in order to be in a position to be heard by the mainstream music culture? And for bands like Mute Math who do follow that path, it's counterproductive to then be marketed as a Christian band. Think of it this way: Would a plumber advertise himself as a "Christian plumber" if he wanted to serve both believers and non-believers? Perhaps, but then, many non-Christians with clogged toilets might not hire him because of that designation. But if he simply presents himself as a "plumber"—still intending to do a great job and

prepared to discuss his faith with any interested clients – he's likely to get more business, earn a better living, and interact with more non-believers. Using "Christian" as an adjective – whether you're a plumber or a musician – is little more than a weapon, used to beat back people who might otherwise be interested in the service or product offered, but upon hearing that it is "Christian" are no longer interested.

Joseph's position is that it's ultimately not a question of content, but marketing:

CM [Christian music] labels need to understand that strong statements of faith, when combined with attractive and interesting music, are not automatic disqualifiers for consideration among non-Christian Americans – provided that the marketing and labeling doesn't frighten them away before being heard. When that happens, they'll have an opportunity to change the way they do business. When they learn to develop and market artists to both those who share their faith and those who don't, functioning as ordinary labels that are part of the mainstream music business, they will eventually realize unprecedented profits – and create a positive environment for bands like Mute Math. When and if that happens, these artists will no longer be put in the position of feeling that they need to sue their labels or leave them. And the labels, instead of standing in the way of artists fulfilling the Great Commission, can instead partner with them in winning a hearing for a generation of talented, and devout, artists.

Ninth, culture will become more important than vision.
This isn't necessarily a Christian media issue, but I do think it's worth mentioning, because it will help set the stage for the kind of innovative and original projects that characterize the future of religious media.

While speaking at a pastor's conference recently, I had the opportunity to meet Dr. Samuel Chand, a consultant for a number of major churches and ministries around the country. Samuel specializes in leadership and management issues, and is a great coach for churches in need of organizational advice and guidance. One of his statements made the entire trip worth it for me: *"Culture is more important than vision."*

Normally, when we talk about churches, ministries and non-profits, we focus on vision. Vision is certainly important – even critical. The right vision sets the direction, tells us where the organization is going and the impact it will have in the future. I'm a big believer in having a powerful vision.

At Cooke Pictures, we've had a number of clients over the years that had powerful visions. Strong leaders with visions that were frankly amazing.

But for a few, despite their vision, the culture in their organizations were toxic.

For a number of reasons, they had created a culture of fear, distrust and strife. Employees disliked each other, they didn't respect the leadership, critics were everywhere and infighting ruled, making it very hard to accomplish anything. The vision was there, but the culture undermined everything.

At the risk of sounding a bit strange, you could literally feel a heaviness when you walked into their offices. It was an oppression that permeated every meeting and every discussion.

Traditional churches and particularly large religious media ministries have often been characterized by great vision. And don't get me wrong – as I've said, vision is critical to the success of an organization. But for some reason, many pastors and church leaders get it backwards – they focus on vision at the expense of the culture that makes that vision happen.

It's a lot like creating a perfect rocket, but neglecting the construction of the launching pad.

It happens because too many pastors believe vision can be realized through the strength of their drive, personality and passion. They believe everyone else will catch on, and once they buy in, the vision will be fulfilled. But your organization's culture is critical to giving birth, nurturing and developing your vision. The culture of your organization is an incubator where vision will grow and mature.

RESULTS AT THE EXPENSE OF RELATIONSHIP

Many of these organization are so focused on the vision they become fanatical about *results*. After all, many think that if you're not getting results, then what's the point?

It's tough to argue with results. In fact – when it comes to religious organizations and non-profits – I wish more were actually focused on results. From evangelism to relief work to fundraising, results are a good thing. But over the years, we've had a few clients that were so results-oriented, it worked against them. Why? Because in an effort to fulfill the vision, they became too focused on results, at the expense of relationship. For instance:

- In order to save a few bucks, they were willing to damage a long-term relationship with an excellent vendor or partner.
- They created an atmosphere of distrust, because they were always nit-picking over issues that didn't really matter.
- They stopped encouraging creative ideas, because a few didn't work out.
- They walked into meetings looking for a fight – frustrated that the vision wasn't being accomplished quickly enough.
- They were more proud of saving money than making an impact or creating excellent work.
- They became budget-oriented instead of people-oriented.

In your well-intentioned pursuit of the vision and of results, don't forget the importance of *relationships*.

BUDGETS AND SCHEDULES ARE IMPORTANT, BUT DON'T LET THEM DRIVE YOUR ORGANIZATION

Not long ago I was on a plane sitting next to a woman that looked to be about 40-years-old. When she discovered I was in the television business, she brightened up and shared with me a story I will never forget. Apparently in high school, she had been a gifted actress and won the lead role in most of the school plays. She naturally wanted to pursue drama in college, and since her parents were fully supportive, they researched a number of university drama programs in the area and started making visits.

Although she grew more excited about an acting career, she said it wasn't long before her passion became somewhat tempered when she realized a couple of unexpected challenges she hadn't considered before. As she explored more and more college drama programs she realized that most serious actors go through undergraduate school, then many to graduate school, and then even as working actors in New York or Los Angeles, continue taking classes for the rest of their career. Then she calculated the price tag of all those classes and came to the conclusion that an acting career would take years to materialize and over time cost a great deal of money.

Essentially she came to the conclusion that her dream would take too long and cost too much money and decided against an acting career.

At that point in our conversation she looked at me with tears in her eyes and said, "Now, twenty years later, I'm a credit manager for a used car lot in Orange County, California. I wake up every morning thinking that if I could only make that decision again, I would work as long as it took and spend any amount of money. Essentially, I gave up my dream and my passion because I thought it would take too long and cost too much, and I've ruined my life."

Don't let budget and schedule determine your destiny.

Remember the importance of values, ideas, creativity and people. Sometimes spending money in the right way creates far more goodwill, motivation and excellence over the long-haul. Stop thinking of ways to squeeze more out of people, and think of ways to empower them to accomplish great things.

I know one church that actually has leadership meetings where they focus on issues like how many health benefits they can take away from employees before they get fed up and quit.

Another held a meeting searching for answers to why their television program was struggling. The CEO opened the meeting with the promise that no one would be fired for being honest, because he wanted the best ideas and suggestions. Nothing they said would be held against them. It was a great meeting. We kicked around some fantastic ideas and developed some powerful solutions. However, one young employee, who was the most excited and offered the best ideas, was fired a few weeks later.

Once again, the status quo won.

I'm sure this didn't originate with me, but *don't fire them – inspire them.* Stop hammering and start helping. If your insecurity is so powerful that you won't change, then get out of the way.

Next generation leaders know that financial problems aren't about money, they're about priorities.

You may spend a few more bucks in the short term, but your long-term results will be far greater than you can imagine.

Culture is more powerful than vision. I've never really heard it put that way, but the minute Samuel said it, it resonated with my own experience.

Is your organization's culture magnetic? Do your employees love coming to work? Do they feel comfortable being completely honest? Are their voices being heard? Have you cultivated an inspiring workplace?

If your organization went out of business tomorrow, would anyone care?

Does your church or ministry provide such a unique experience that your congregation or ministry supporters would be upset if it didn't exist? Does your church or non-profit treat its employees so incredibly well that those workers would not be able to find another employer to treat them as well? Does your church or organization create such compelling emotional connections in your community or support base that they would fail to find another organization that would forge as strong an emotional and spiritual bond? Is the ministry or humanitarian work you're doing so effective and making such a difference that the world would be worse off if you stopped? Have you impacted so many people that it's tough to go a week without someone commenting on how much your organization has meant to their lives?

These are all questions worth asking – questions you *should* be asking.

More than any other generation in history, the millennial generation wants their job to have meaning. No matter how important, original or significant your vision, if you can't create a culture in your organization that fosters creativity, innovation, teamwork, and fun, it's not worth doing. Because no matter how great the vision, if the culture doesn't work, the vision will fail.

Ten, Christian media must transcend the marketplace.
As I look at Christian media today, I see an industry built on what people *want*, not necessarily on what they *need*. There are a number of reasons for this dilemma. Some would point to budget restrictions and say they do what they have to do to

keep their ministries afloat; others would say these media ministries are just adapting to the culture.

> **RELIGION CANNOT BECOME SO OF THE MARKET THAT IT LOSES ITS UNIQUE SELLING PROPOSITION: ITS ABILITY TO RAISE US ABOVE THE MARKET.**
> – MARA EINSTEIN, *BRANDS OF FAITH*

While we present our message in terms of a powerful and compelling story, while we use terms like "branding" to explain perception or "marketing" to reach the widest possible audience, never think that the Christian faith is just another *lifestyle choice*. This isn't a soft drink, a computer or a car we're talking about here.

I mentioned earlier that in our well meaning effort to relate to the culture, I'm getting some interesting comments from a younger generation about many contemporary churches today. When church looks like just another metal building, concert arena or shopping mall, we've lost something of it's meaning.

Many people my age grew up in a traditional church that was lifeless and dull, so we tried to integrate our worship with music we love and styles we identify with. But today we might be experiencing a different swing in the pendulum.

While torn jeans and exposed shirt-tails are certainly a visual indicator of the trend, for me it's much more than how a pastor dresses. I'm looking at the overall experience. When the worship experience becomes too casual (especially in attitude), where is the mystery? I really think there should be a place for transcendence in worship, and to be honest, I don't see much of it in churches today.

Liturgical churches have continued their traditions right down to the incense, and I find that somewhat appealing – and apparently so do thousands of Christians moving toward that tradition. Certainly the ultimate goal is a powerful encounter with the divine, and playing "dress up" doesn't accomplish that. But are we missing something in contemporary worship?

> **I DON'T THINK A WHOLE LOT OF PEOPLE CARE ABOUT WHAT KIND OF MUSIC YOU HAVE OR HOW YOU SHAPE A SERVICE. THEY WANT A PLACE WHERE GOD IS TAKEN SE-RIOUSLY, AND WHERE THEY ARE TAKEN SERIOUSLY.**
> – EUGENE PETERSON, THEOLOGIAN AND PASTOR

People are saved in all kinds ways and in many different situations – from a high youth group to prison cells and night-clubs. But shouldn't pastors and church leaders at least aim for a more transcendent experience? Should church look and feel like the local mall?

WHY STRATEGY MATTERS

In a chapter that deals with mixing media, targeting niche audiences, media response and digital choices I would be remiss of me not to discuss the importance of *strategy*.

In the business and non-profit world, there are a number of people and companies that deal with strategy: strategic planners, strategy consultants and media strategists. But what is strategy and why does it really matter?

According to William Duggan who wrote, *Strategic Intuition*, the word "tactics" came into use roughly around 1600 and referred to battlefield planning. It wasn't until around 1810 the idea of "strategy" appeared. And everything changed when Carl Von Clausewitz began using strategy in battle.

Strategy is about the choices that affect outcomes. While there have been volumes written on strategy, at its most elementary level, it can be broken down to three basic steps:

1) Figure out where you are (Point A)
2) Decide where you want to be (Point B)
3) Create a plan to get from A to B

It's incredibly simple, but it's surprising how few people – particularly in media and ministry – actually take the time to consider these steps and determine the ideal solution. If you're involved in communicating a message, then you need to understand how it works.

HAVING A PLAN TO REACH YOUR AUDIENCE WITH THE RIGHT MESSAGE IS CRITICAL

Whatever the challenge you're facing – the strategy (or lack thereof) – that got you in this sorry situation, won't be the same strategy that gets you out. Will Rogers once said, "When you find yourself in a hole, the first thing to do is to stop digging."

I'm shocked at the number of people that just keep doing the same thing year after year as if the direction of the ministry, audience numbers, response, income – whatever, will magically change. But getting from point A to point B doesn't happen by accident. It happens by implementing a well thought out plan.

And by the way – when it comes to churches – changing graphics, adding cool music and lighting effects or dumping the choir robes is not a strategy. That's just re-arranging deck chairs on the Titanic. *You need to fundamentally rethink what story your church or ministry is trying to tell, what that means to your audience, how to connect with that audience, and why it's absolutely urgent they respond right now.*
One major media ministry was convinced their shrinking audience and disappearing donations could be solved by updating their graphics. Another believed that a better program opening would turn their ministry around.

Better graphic styles and a more contemporary opening can be important, but they are only pieces of a much larger overall strategy.

The 21st century is changing everything about how we communicate. Yesterday it was about dumping the same message on the mass audience because there was no other choice. Today, it's about making a "connection" – the kind of connection that not only makes an audience want to hear what you have to say, but furthermore makes them want to respond.

Understanding that connection is a critical step in finding – and keeping – your audience.

CHAPTER TWELVE
EMBRACE AMBIGUITY:
APPRECIATING THE MYSTERY OF LIFE

> **THE TEST OF A FIRST-RATE INTELLIGENCE IS THE ABILITY TO HOLD TWO OPPOSED IDEAS IN THE MIND AT THE SAME TIME, AND STILL RETAIN THE ABILITY TO FUNCTION.**
> – F. SCOTT FITZGERALD, *THE GREAT GATSBY*

> **NEUROSIS IS THE INABILITY TO TOLERATE AMBIGUITY.**
> – SIGMUND FREUD

As we dive into the brave new world of media, I have to mention the importance of being comfortable with ambiguity. We are now in the middle of what philosophers call post-modernism. One of the hallmarks of the modern mind – especially during the last hundred years – is certainty. The rise of modern science made us believe that everything, given enough time, can be proven. We came to see our world as something measurable, concrete and exact.

But we've discovered that life isn't as exact as we thought. We discovered science doesn't necessarily hold the promise we thought it did. Marriages still fail, violence is on the rise and poverty is rampant. There are too many questions about our origins, purpose and destiny that science has failed to answer.

Life is wonderful, but messy.

As a pastor's son, I attended more funerals by age twelve than most people attend in a lifetime. My dad conducted funerals for children, teenagers, young adults – many people who had no reason to die and every reason to live.

> **AGAIN, I SAW THAT THE RACE IS NOT TO THE SWIFT...**
> **NOR FAVOR TO THE SKILLFUL; BUT TIME AND CHANCE**
> **HAPPEN TO THEM ALL.**
>   – ECCLESIASTES 9:11 (NRSV)

To reach the next generation, we have to create programming that acknowledges that we have to accept the mystery of life, realize it's not always fair, and we don't have all the answers.

If post-modern thought can help us, this is perhaps it's strongest argument: while we worship the God of Truth, day to day living isn't necessarily about certainty, being right, or finding all the answers.

Life is more about asking the right questions.

From the beginning, we have been creatures of choice. We are not ruled by instincts, robotic instructions or programming. We have free will – we can choose. But within that choice is the great paradox.

Choice means that we are free to do evil as well as good. Choice means that we live in a world where birth, life and growth are balanced by decay, disease and destruction. Choice means the responsibility to do the right thing – not the license to do what we please. Choice means that true redemption is in life's struggles.

CHOICE MEANS AMBIGUITY

Listen to the evening news for very long and you'll see the parade of people demanding "rights" for everything you can possibly imagine. On camera, these people are quick to talk about *rights*, but not so quick to talk about *responsibilities*. Understanding ambiguity is to take responsibility for our own lives regardless of what happens to us. Accepting ambiguity may be our greatest act of faith.

In his book, *The Answer to How is Yes*, Peter Block explains:

> Problems that count need to be respected before they will reveal themselves to us. The focus on tools, answers and problem solving keeps them in hiding, because we will just revert to the solutions, which are more easily implemented. The push for concrete action is exactly what sidetracks our dreams and postpones until tomorrow what needs to be addressed today. In the movie "Shakespeare in Love," one of the characters is constantly in trouble, and when pressed to the wall on when he is going to repay his debt, he answers, "it's a mystery to me." It could be seen as a clever way of stalling, but perhaps it was a genuine expression of faith.

Bookstores and religious media ministries churn out a constant stream of books providing easy answers. Go to the self-help or business section – or turn on Christian radio and TV – and you'll find a multitude of titles such as *The Three Easy Steps to Financial Success, Living at Your Best, Successful Families,* or *The Secrets of a Strong Marriage.* I've read many of these books over the years, and I have to admit that I'm still not as financially secure as I'd like, I could still be living better, my family does dumb things, and my wife Kathleen and I continue to have our spats. I've discovered the search for easy answers is a futile effort that usually leads to failure and frustration.

Yes, much of the information in these books is solid, useful information that can really help people. But life isn't about finding easy answers – life is about asking the right questions.

When you stop looking for easy answers in the media, you'll begin to recognize a far bigger picture.

Life doesn't always make sense, and neither do audiences. I often joke that if you could figure out what audiences *actually* want, you'd be a billionaire overnight. Every season,

great programs are cancelled, while stupid, insipid programming flourishes. I had dinner with a major network executive
last night and he was sharing his frustration at the difficulty
in finding new programs. His network had spent hundreds
of millions over the past year on pilots, in what turned out
to be a mostly failed attempt at creating a successful new TV
season. Sometimes, no matter how hard we work, the project
still fails.

Recently while watching the news, I saw a father weeping because his thirteen-year-old daughter decided to take
the family car on a joyride, lost control and killed two young
children. She came from a good family and was an excellent
student; her parents loved her and raised her by the book.
There was no rational reason for her impulse, but she made
a choice and as a result, three families were shattered. As
I watched that weeping father, I realized there are no easy
answers in life.

> **I HAVE SEEN EVERYTHING IN THIS WORLD, AND I TELL
> YOU, IT IS ALL USELESS. IT IS LIKE CHASING THE WIND.
> YOU CAN'T STRAIGHTEN OUT WHAT IS CROOKED; YOU
> CAN'T COUNT THINGS THAT AREN'T THERE.**
> – ECCLESIASTES 1:14-15 (NRSV)

If you think the Bible is a story of fairy tales for wimps
– think again. The Old Testament book of Ecclesiastes was
written by a man who had seen everything, been everywhere
and owned as much as any man on earth. He had enjoyed
everything life had to offer and all he saw was emptiness and
vanity. He understood the difference between a life of true understanding and a life devoid of purpose and meaning. It's a
book that deals with the reality of living without holding back
or cutting corners.

Film critic and professor of Theology and Culture at Fuller Seminary, Robert Johnston, addresses this topic in his book *Useless Beauty: Ecclesiastes Through The Lens of Contemporary Film*:

> Medieval Old Testament scholars called Ecclesiastes one of the Bible's two most dangerous books. (The other was the Song of Songs with its overt sensuality). Though its trenchant observations on life reveal a fragile joy – a useless beauty – its paragraphs also brim over with a cynicism and even a despair that seem out of place in the Bible's grand narrative. But at the end of this despair, the writer of Ecclesiastes also offers us hope. He offers real wisdom instead of easy answers. Life is not a manageable project or a test to be taken. We can find small joys everyday if we have eyes of faith. We can find meaning if we search for a greater purpose. And perhaps most important, we need to realize that life is a great gift.

In M. Night Shyamalan's movie, "Signs," a small town minister has lost his faith and abandoned his calling because of the senseless death of his wife. But as the story unfolds, he discovers fragments of meaning in normally inconsequential events. Things others never noticed begin to have enormous meaning for this former pastor. The Bible says now we see in part – and for the pastor in the movie, the parts begin to make sense. Finally, as he was able to set aside his bitterness and anger, he began to piece together the meaning and rediscovered his faith.

So what can we make of this idea of ambiguity? How can we face a world without all the answers when we have deep questions and yearnings that we don't understand? When the Bible holds the ultimate answers to life, how do we, in good conscience, engage the audience with more questions?

As Peter Block suggests in the above quote, we need to stop looking for simple answers and start asking bigger questions.

For things that matter, you'll find the real answer deep inside the question. It's interesting that when the people of the

New Testament asked Jesus questions, he turned right back to them with another question. Great teachers and philosophers throughout history have done the same thing, because they understood the power of questions and how they can be the key to real understanding. Life is complicated. Life is difficult. Life is not neat and organized. The obvious answers we're looking for aren't always quick and easy.

LIFE IS ABOUT THE JOURNEY, NOT THE DESTINATION

We see this phrase written on cute motivational posters but often underestimate its real power. Stop waiting to arrive. As a young man I spent most of my life "waiting to finish." Driving in the car on summer vacation, I couldn't wait to get there; in school, I couldn't wait to get out of class; at work, I couldn't wait to finish the project. Then one day I realized that I've spent most of my life waiting for something and never enjoying the process. I was missing most of life's greatest moments while waiting for something better.

NEVER REPLACE *WHAT'S NOW* FOR *WHAT'S NEXT*

Nothing reveals that frustration as much as watching your children grow. Today, one of our daughters is married and the other is finishing college, and it's amazing to realize that only yesterday they were sitting on my lap telling me what they wanted for Christmas. Kathleen and I watch home videos and wish we could go back, just for a day. They grew up so fast and I wish I had been in the moment and relished those early days a little more. My life is here and now. My family is here and now. My marriage is here and now. My career is here and now. The journey is taking place everyday. Stop looking for the finish line and enjoy the race.

Dr. Larry Poland, founder of Mastermedia International in Hollywood, puts it this way: *Stop rowing and start sailing.*

Poland describes most people as struggling against the wind, rowing, giving it their best but wearing themselves out in the process. They want to control their direction and force the boat to go a particular way.

Experienced sailors know that if they just relax a little, they can steer but let the wind do the real work. Sure you might not go in the exact direction you prefer, and you might even wander off course a little, but knowing how to steer allows you to arrive at the same destination while enjoying the ride.

Sit back, relax a little and accept the mystery. Perhaps how or when you get there doesn't matter quite as much as you thought. The writer of Ecclesiastes knew that we all end up at the same place – as dust. The only difference is how we enjoy the journey.

Somehow, that's the message the next generation is looking for right now. They've been immersed in media and there's no going back. By one account, 70 percent of day care centers in the United States have the television on for at least two hours every day, and how many parents use the TV as a babysitter?

As a result, we're facing a generation that is highly skeptical of an easy fix. They know an infomercial isn't the ultimate answer to their problems, they view TV commercials as entertainment and aren't satisfied or challenged by a simplistic sermon. They understand that life is complicated and they are far more comfortable *participating* in a conversation than *listening* to a lecture.

The question is, can we respond through the media? Can we embrace ambiguity and create programming that truly engages? It doesn't mean we water down or compromise the message – it means being honest about our doubts, our fears and our questions. The truth won't make us *less* credible, it will make us *more* credible.

Don't stop bold preaching and teaching. Don't even stop writing "how to" books and sermons. But understand that when you engage the audience in the *questions*, you form a powerful partnership and far deeper relationship. Great programming provides both – it starts with the questions and helps the audience find their own answers.

This isn't about compromising our message or doubting the fact that God can transform lives. It's not a question of *what we know*, it's a question of *how we relate*. By engaging your audience with questions, you're inviting them to be part of the discovery process. And if we're honest, we have to admit that most of the really tough questions in life can't be answered this side of Heaven anyway.

Our programming can either celebrate the mystery and ambiguity of life or we can continue to pretend we have all the answers. I can't change the weather or other people's behavior. I can't add a single day to my life or force anyone to follow Jesus. If we can reflect that honesty in the media, we'll make a powerful connection.

As a believer in God, I believe in absolute Truth. But I also believe that He's in control, and for me to always demand answers is to assume His role. I've decided to sit back and let Him be God, and let me be me.

Be honest. Be authentic. Be real.

CHAPTER THIRTEEN:
WHERE DO WE GO FROM HERE?

If by now you think I'm anti-*traditional* media or even anti-*religious* media, you've missed my point. I'm anti-*bad* media. I'm anti-*stupid* media and anti-*pointless* media. Entertainment, information, education, ministry, inspiration – regardless of what type of media programming you create – I'm against media that isn't honest and authentic, doesn't accomplish a purpose, doesn't express your values, and doesn't find an audience.

Traditional media will always be with us – after all, I may spend my days on the computer and iPhone, but Kathleen and I still cuddle up in front of my widescreen TV (my Christmas gift to her of course) for a good movie.

The key is finding the right media mix for the right message and the right audience.

If anything, this book should make you far less TV, radio, or web centric – and make you realize that reaching the next generation will take a strategic mix of multiple media options.

I'm not even against preaching on TV. Some of our favorite clients at Cooke Pictures are pastors and ministry leaders, but they all recognize the limitations of talking heads, and work with us to explore different approaches and visual ideas. These are men and women who understand that what worked in the past won't necessarily work in the future, and to reach a visual generation, it's time to start making changes.

THERE IS NO MAGIC BULLET

You've just read about what's wrong with religious media, what's changing the media business and a glimpse of the future. But if I could leave you with a single thought, it would be this: *there is no magic bullet.*

In turbulent times of change, the old rules don't apply, the new rules aren't written, and the current rules are changing.

There are no simple answers.

But there is a bright side. What I find so fascinating about this moment in time, is the fact that when it comes to navigating the digital media world, Hollywood movie studios, major TV networks, and global entertainment companies are all in the same boat as a small church in Milwaukee, a media ministry in Dallas and *you*. As is typical during changing times like these, there is little empirical data available, but experience is a good teacher.

> ONE SCHOLAR HAS GONE SO FAR AS TO SAY THAT "CONSUMERISM HAS BECOME A PREDOMINANT CHARACTERISTIC OF AMERICAN RELIGION." HOWEVER, IT DOESN'T HAVE TO BE THE DEFINING CHARACTERISTIC. IT CAN BE A CHARACTERISTIC MEANS FOR BRINGING PEOPLE TO FAITH, WITHOUT BECOMING THE FAITH ITSELF.
>
> – MARA EINSTEIN, *BRANDS OF FAITH*

Here are my recommendations in the context of the current media landscape and how it could impact your organization. I would encourage you to meet with your team and make sure they understand these important principles:

1) Don't overreact.
Too many organizations panic during times of transition and make decisions they come to regret. Don't assume the worst and don't act out of fear or frustration. This is the time for thoughtful reflection, creativity, and strategy – not a time to freak out.

2) Refocus on your mission.
Too many churches and ministry organizations find success, grow and then lose sight of their original mission. That's usually because they become distracted with how to *pay* for their mission. So let's go back to the beginning. Why did you start this organization? What are your priorities? Never lose sight of your original purpose during challenging times. It will help keep you focused. Keep your results in front of your congregation or donors. Especially during times of transition, donors want to know where their money is going, so keep them updated. Let them know how your work is impacting lives. Remind them frequently that you're accomplishing exactly what you said you would. As far as the donors are concerned, unless they know about what you've been doing, it doesn't exist.

3) Streamline carefully.
I always advocate a lean, mean, mission machine. So what are "convenience" areas in the organization that have grown fat? Did you start additional mission outreaches for the wrong reasons? Do they really compliment and reflect your brand identity? Rarely do I find a church, ministry or non-profit that hasn't made the mistake of adding at least one program or outreach that's very different from the founding purpose of their organization. Don't hack, but start looking at areas and

departments that don't really reflect your calling, aren't getting results or confuse donors about your mission. That's usually the places to start trimming.

And keep that streamlining mindset prominent throughout your organization, and start with the employee manuals or handbooks. I've seen employee manuals for religious and non-profit organizations that were literally hundreds of pages long. How many rules do you really need to do great work?

It's interesting that for years, Nordstrom has been considered a brilliantly run business. So I checked their employee manual, and to my surprise it has one page. On that page it says:

"Rule # 1 – 'Use your good judgment in all situations. There will be no additional rules.'"

Point taken.

4) If finances get tight, start saving with materials, not people.
If you get to the point where you need to make serious cuts, before you start laying off anyone, let's look at materials first. Could you use less expensive paper? Could you save on your light bill? Because Prestonwood Church in Dallas is such a large facility, Pastor Jack Graham has actually appointed a staff member in charge of energy conservation. It was such a bold and unusual move, the story has been written up in the national news. Jack discovered the enormous savings potential by simply taking a proactive approach to conserving energy. Likewise are there other areas (office supplies, vehicles, insurance carriers, phone and IT services, etc.) where serious cost comparisons could save you money? One small municipality in the Midwest saved $25,000 a year in energy costs just by turning off the City Hall computers at night. Things that seem minor can really add up.

5) Don't cut your lifelines.
Never forget that other than God of course, your congregation and/or donors are your source – and your media outreaches

are your lifeline to that source. A few years ago a couple of national media ministries cut as many as 1/3 of their TV stations to save money – without realizing they were cutting 1/3 of their donor contact. Even after a few years, they have yet to recover. It's important to constantly evaluate results, make changes, and respond accordingly, but be very careful about drastic media changes just to save money. Your most vital links to your donors are your media – radio, TV, website, direct mail, etc. Be sure you understand the relationship.

Radio and TV are about perception, direct mail is about results

One national media leader described it like this: "Because of radio and TV people know who we are, and because of direct mail, they support us." TV won't generate much income by itself, and you can't expand your audience and donors with just direct mail. Working together is the key. One can't work effectively without the other. The only exception is, at a local level, where mail may be your only option. In that case, focus your message, target the audience and be as original and efficient as possible.

6) With radio and TV, work your media buy.
When and where your radio or TV program is broadcast can make a dramatic difference in response. Don't just cut your stations at random like the earlier example, but constantly tweak and adjust to make sure your program is reaching the right audience. Too many organizations hire media buyers and then never hear from them again. When was the last time you had a presentation from your media buyer with recommendations and new ideas? A good media buyer should be proactive – constantly looking for the best placement for your program. It is a continuous process. Once they get an available time slot, they shouldn't stop working for you. Press them. Challenge their placement decisions. Make them keep earning their money.

7) Be open to change.

Too many churches and ministries go through difficult times because they're unwilling to experiment and try something new. Some fear the longtime donors will get upset if they change the program. Others are insecure and still others just can't get beyond their self-imposed box. You'll never know how far you can reach unless you try. Especially during times of radical change you often have no choice.

8) Don't change too often.

Having just said, "Be open to change," I also know some organizations that won't stick with any plan long enough for it to work. I believe in the power of change but innovation needs time to succeed. Make changes, but don't let fear haunt you with self-doubt. With one former client we would spend all day in a creative meeting laying out a new strategy, but by the time I flew home, I would have a phone message saying he'd changed his mind. He was consumed with insecurity and self-doubt and couldn't rustle up the courage to commit. As a result, his ministry has yet to reach its full potential.

9) Sell the change to your congregation, audience and/or donors.

Don't just make changes and expect everyone to be on board. Your listeners or viewers need to know your heart, and understand why change is happening. Joyce Meyer did this brilliantly when she rebranded a number of years ago. After spending months sharing why she felt reaching a new generation was critical, her donors responded with great excitement. Don't leave your donors in the dark. Give them a vision, allow them to participate, and give them a sense of ownership in the mission. And don't forget your employees. Everyone reacts differently to change, so make sure you've discussed it with your team, given them the information they need, and listened to their ideas and concerns. Making your employees part of the process reaps enormous benefits.

10) Keep growing personally.
Once you discover the over-arching brand story that describes your ministry, it's only the beginning. You should be constantly searching for how that story can impact this culture. Are you reading books, magazines, and newspapers, watching TV and movies, and engaging the culture? I listen to some pastors and ministry leaders who appear to be trapped somewhere in the 70's or 80's. Don't chase trends, but study them to see where the culture is going. There's an old advertising saying that: "Once product sales are down, it's too late to advertise."

Telling your story should be an ongoing process – and you should always be looking for original and innovative ways to engage. If you're telling the same stories or preaching from the same notes you made 10 years ago, then you're behind the curve. The great thing about the Bible is that it answers the "now" questions of life, and far too many pastors are answering yesterday's questions.

11) Branding is more important than ever because it's about trust.
During difficult times, organizations need a solid account of "brand equity" built up with donors or customers. When times are tough or uncertain, they're more likely to give if they trust you. So don't let up on your brand. This is the time to invest even more in building your brand and fostering a sense of trust between you and your donors.

One of the major reasons for the intense growth of branding as an industry and focus, is its connection to *meaning*. Major companies now realize that business isn't just about generating revenue, it's about meaning. People are hungry to make a difference, and if you can associate real meaning with what you do and how you do it, you will significantly increase your chances of making a strong connection with your audience.

12) Optimize search engines.
In the digital universe, your name is only as good as Google says it is. When you type your organization's name into Google or other search engines, does good or bad stuff come up? Or nothing? While it's tricky, results can be changed and improved. Are others blogging about you? Are you putting out good things on the web? If you have bloggers in your church or among your supporters, encourage them to regularly post about how your organization or your teaching has impacted their lives. Positive stuff is important. Don't lose customers or donors searching for you on the web – work on your search results.

The future is about *findability*. Google is the home page for millions of people. I have no doubt the vast majority of Internet users go online for the primary purpose of searching. Therefore, in an online world, your ability to be found is a very significant issue. Stop thinking of search in the sense of looking for something concrete or lost. Today, search isn't just about finding the answer to this or that. *It's about exploration. It's about discovery. It's about stumbling onto things we didn't know we needed or even existed.*

In the old days, I created multiple email folders to organize my email messages in terms of clients and projects, but with the advent of better and better search capabilities, I've deleted all those mailboxes and now I just search for what I need. Search will continue to have huge implications for the future of media.

13) Direct mail still works.
In fact, direct mail is still a larger industry than all online advertising and marketing put together. But today, it's important to make sure your direct mail is driving people to your website. Get more bang for your buck and focus on developing both marketing avenues together. Direct mail is now. Online is the future.

14) Don't be afraid to ask for financial support.
Sadly, most Christian radio and TV ministries fall into either end of the spectrum; ministries either ask for money all the time or they don't ask at all. Be honest. Put the need out there and ask people to partner with you. If you do it with taste and class, urgency is just fine. People actually appreciate it when you're being straight with them, and if you have a financial need, let them know it.

15) Tell better stories.
Branding is the art of surrounding a product, person or organization with a compelling story. As novelist Ursula LaGuin wrote, "There have been great societies that did not use the wheel, but there have been no societies that did not tell stories." Stories are a foundational, core aspect of our being. We share meaning through stories and their power elevates us to new levels of accomplishment. It's no surprise that the Bible isn't simply a book of theology, doctrine or dogma; it's a book of powerful stories that have been changing lives for thousands of years.

ARE YOU CONSUMERS OR REAL PARTICIPANTS?
– GRAFFITI AT THE SORBONNE, PARIS, 1968

Be encouraged. The church has survived persecution, abandonment, and neglect. The coming media revolution won't *stop* the message; and for those watching the signs, it can help *advance* the message. From this point on, how we choose to connect with the culture will make a dramatic difference in the effectiveness of our mission.

The new media generation is about stories and conversations, not sermons and lectures. It's about popping the bubble of religious media and embracing the secular audience. To impact the culture we need to engage, not boycott or criticize.

I'm calling Christian communicators to a movement. A revolution that will change the way we engage the culture and create media.

Join me, as we navigate the digital divide.

HOW THIS BOOK WAS PUBLISHED

Because much of the information in *The Last TV Evangelist* was about current and future technology, it was important for me that the book reach the marketplace as quickly as possible. When my agent, Bucky Rosenbaum, and I spoke to various traditional publishers, they all agreed that through conventional publishing methods, it could take up to a year to get the finished book edited, designed, printed, and shipped to stores.

I realized that wouldn't work because even as Bucky was talking to publishers, I was updating information as new technology became available. We needed a publisher that was as original and innovative as the media revolution this book describes.

That's when we met Stan Jantz and Bruce Bickel at Conversantlife.com. Stan, Bruce and their team were developing a collaborative publishing model that utilized "on demand publishing" technology as a way to create a new template for reaching audiences faster and more efficiently.

As a non-traditional publisher, Conversantlife.com didn't pay hefty advances or have big budgets for conventional advertising campaigns. But they *did* have a unique understanding of how to use the web for creating conversations, developing word of mouth marketing, and connecting with conferences.

Perhaps more than that, *they were passionate about the project*. From the first draft Bucky sent to Stan, he was remarkably excited and felt that this project needed to happen. There were bugs to work out because the process is new and the technology still isn't perfect, but if we were going to put our money where our mouth is, this was the direction we needed to move.

As a result, we were able to reduce our publishing schedule from the year it took my previous publisher to create my book, *Branding Faith*, to three months with the book you're now reading.

The media revolution is happening, and the book you're holding right now is an example of how the publishing paradigm is responding to that change.

Phil Cooke, November 2008

COOKEPICTURES

Tell Your Story More Effectively in a Media Driven Culture

A new media conversation is happening in the culture. It's about the transition from the traditional world to the digital world. It's about immediacy, connection, and influence. While traditional media still makes the money and wields the power, a powerful new paradigm is emerging.

Television may be the king of now, but digital media is the king of tomorrow. At Cooke Pictures, we speak both languages – helping you strengthen your current media programming, while working to create the future. Navigating that change is exactly what we do through creative ideas, production, branding, and media strategy.

If you're waiting for digital media to become cost-effective, you're already being left behind. The new digital transition is not about income, it's about influence. While traditional media is concerned about making money, the new digital pioneers are concerned about change.

If your goal is to impact the culture, then our goal is to help you have a disproportionate influence in making that happen.

Producing | Media Branding | Consultation

Cooke Pictures is one of the most successful media companies and respected consultants for faith-based | non-profit media.

Contact the creative team at Cooke Pictures today, and stop worrying about the future and start creating it.

COOKEPICTURES.COM

THE CHANGE REVOLUTION
AT PHILCOOKE.COM

"CHANGE, WHEN IT COMES, CRACKS EVERYTHING OPEN."
– DOROTHY ALLISON

Change is here, and change is happening whether we like it or not.

My online blog at philcooke.com is about the change happening at the intersection of media, faith, and culture. The rules are being transformed, and if we're going to create media that matters, we need to understand the revolution. What fuels your passion? Producing projects that make an impact? Movies, TV, and digital media that matter? Whatever it is, this is the place to discuss it.

You can link this blog to your site via our RSS News Feed or a simple link to our homepage. And sign up for our free, monthly e-mail newsletter, *Ideas for the Change Revolution*. It's a great source of research, creative ideas, and techniques from Phil Cooke regarding media and culture change, and how you can make that change work for you.

I believe we all have a purpose. But if we're ever going to discover our destiny, we need to understand change, and how to achieve long-lasting, revolutionary transformation in every area of our lives. Because if we can change ourselves, we can change the world.

Join us for The Change Revolution...

PHILCOOKE.COM

Conversant Media Group

Conversant Media Group is the creative force behind *Conversantlife.com*, a content rich new-media website that encourages conversations about faith and culture through expert blogs, social news, video, podcasts, and community participation.

Conversant Media Group utilizes a "collaborative publishing" business model and digital print technologies to produce engaging books offered in traditional print as well as various electronic formats.

www.ConversantMediaGroup.com

www.ConversantLife.com

Printed in the United States
220916BV00002B/7/P